Table of Contents

How to Use Llewellyn's *Witches' Datebook* 4
The Urban Pagan *by Dorothy Morrison* 6
Magical Connections *by Wren Walker* 9
Handfasting *by Jami Shoemaker* 14
Lunar Spellworking *by Estelle Daniels* 18
Gingerbread: A Witch's Love Story *by Thea Bloom* 26
January 32
February 40
March 48
April 58
May 66
June 75
July 84
August 92
September 101
October 110
November 118
December 127
About the Authors 138
Telephone Pages 140

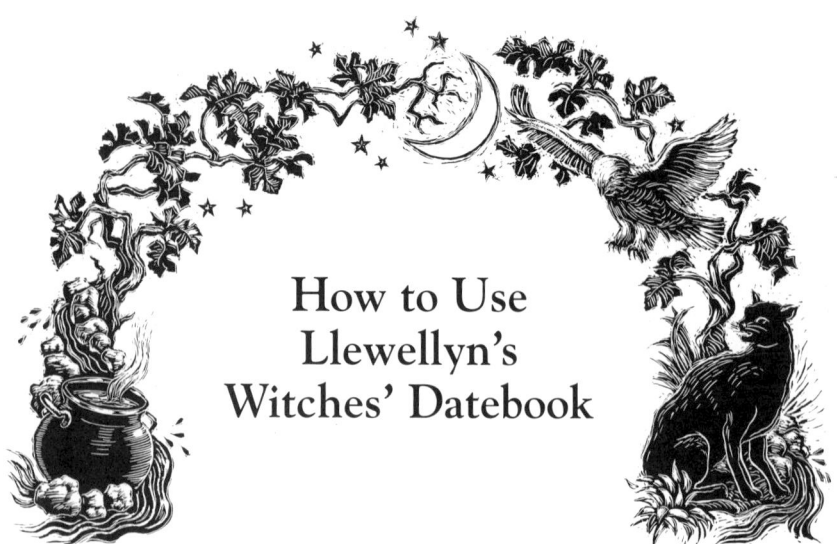

How to Use Llewellyn's Witches' Datebook

Welcome to Llewellyn's *Witches' Datebook 2002*. This datebook was designed especially for Witches, Pagans, and magical people. Use it to plan sabbat celebrations, magic, Full Moon rites, and even dentist appointments! Below is a symbol key to some of the features of this datebook. In addition, *there is a symbol key on the inside back cover flap of this book* that you can leave open next to the book for easy reference.

MOON QUARTERS: The Moon's cycle is divided into four quarters, which are noted in the calendar pages along with their exact times. When the Moon changes quarter, both quarters are listed, as well as the time of the change. In addition, a symbol for the new quarter is placed where the numeral for the date usually appears.

MOON IN THE SIGNS: Approximately every two-and-a-half days the Moon moves from one zodiac sign to the next. The sign that the Moon is in at the beginning of the day (midnight Eastern Standard Time) is noted next to the quarter listing. If the Moon changes signs that day, there will be a notation saying "☽ enters" followed by the symbol for the sign it is entering.

MOON VOID-OF-COURSE: Just before the Moon enters a new sign it will make one final aspect (angular relationship) to another planet. Between that last aspect and the entrance of the Moon into the next sign it is said to be void-of-course. Activities begun when the Moon is void rarely come to fruition, or they turn out very differently than planned.

Llewellyn's Witches' Datebook 2002

Featuring

Art by Kathleen Edwards. Text by Thea Bloom, Estelle Daniels, Marguerite Elsbeth, Anna Franklin, Yasmine Galenorn, Magenta Griffith, Lady Gyngere of the Grove, Edain McCoy, Dorothy Morrison, Jami Shoemaker, K. D. Spitzer, and Wren Walker

ISBN 0-7387-0039-8

Llewellyn's *Witches' Datebook 2002* ©2001 by Llewellyn Worldwide. P.O. Box 64383 Dept. 0-7387-0039-8, St. Paul, MN 55164. All rights reserved. No part of this publication may be reproduced in any form without the permission of the publisher except for quotations used in critical reviews.

Editing/design by K. M. Brielmaier

Cover illustration and interior art © 2001 by Kathleen Edwards

Cover design by Anne Marie Garrison, color by Lynne Menturweck

Art direction by Lynne Menturweck

Moon sign and phase data by Astro Communications Services

PLANETARY MOVEMENT: When a planet or asteroid moves from one sign into another, this change (called an *ingress*) is noted on the calendar pages with the exact time. The Moon and Sun are considered planets in this case. The planets (except for the Sun and Moon) can also appear to move backward as seen from the Earth. This is called a *planetary retrograde*, and is noted on the calendar pages with the symbol ℞. When the planet begins to move forward, or direct, again, it is marked D, and the time is also noted.

PLANTING AND HARVESTING DAYS: The best days for planting and harvesting are noted on the calendar pages with a seedling icon (planting) and a scythe icon (harvesting).

TIME ZONE CHANGES: The times and dates of all astrological phenomena in this datebook are based on Eastern Standard Time (EST). If you live outside of EST, you will need to make the following changes: Pacific Standard Time (PST) subtract three hours; Mountain Standard Time (MST) subtract two hours; Central Standard Time (CST) subtract one hour; Alaska/Hawaii subtract five hours; and during Daylight Saving Time add an hour.

Planets
- ☉ Sun
- ☽ Moon
- ☿ Mercury
- ♀ Venus
- ♂ Mars
- ♃ Jupiter
- ♄ Saturn
- ♅ Uranus
- ♆ Neptune
- ♇ Pluto
- ⚷ Chiron
- ⚳ Ceres
- ⚴ Pallas
- ⚵ Juno
- ⚶ Vesta

Signs
- ♈ Aries
- ♉ Taurus
- ♊ Gemini
- ♋ Cancer
- ♌ Leo
- ♍ Virgo
- ♎ Libra
- ♏ Scorpio
- ♐ Sagittarius
- ♑ Capricorn
- ♒ Aquarius
- ♓ Pisces

Motion
- ℞ Retrograde
- D Direct

1st Quarter/New Moon ☽
2nd Quarter ☾
3rd Quarter/Full Moon: ☺
4th Quarter ☽

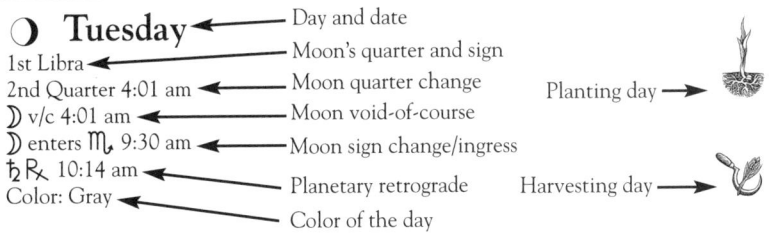

The Urban Pagan
by Dorothy Morrison

Charms. Spells. Ritual magic. Just the sound of these words evokes visions of oak-lined groves, cool earth, babbling brooks, and herb-sprinkled forests. We can almost see the circle of stones, hear the drums, and feel the magic take root. One more stretch of the imagination and our ancestors are there, too, pounding away with mortars and pestles, dancing to Nature's rhythm, and—with a bit of this and a touch of that—weaving their magic in shape and form until it becomes a living, breathing entity. It isn't so hard to imagine. Especially in that sort of setting.

Today, though, most Pagans don't have access to undisturbed woodlands. In fact, some of them don't even have backyards. They live in metropolitan areas filled with skyscrapers, concrete, and ribbons of interstate that twirl into infinity. They live in suburban areas conquered by housing developments, apartments, and condos. Some of them even live in areas that haven't seen a tree in years—and the closest thing to a natural stream is the man-made fountain that spurts and flows in the center of the town square. That being the case, how do they practice their nature-based religions? More to the point, how do they even get their magic off the ground?

They do exactly what their ancestors did. They use their heads and take advantage of the resources at hand.

In ancient times, for example, it was simply more expedient to worship outdoors. For one thing, it saved time, and—since our ancestors weren't privy to our modern-day conveniences—time was a very valuable commodity, indeed. Constructing a building meant using up hours that they just couldn't afford to spare. Instead, they braved the elements and practiced outdoors. Not only were forests plentiful and fairly private, most folks either lived close to wooded areas or owned property that contained them. It was all a matter of common sense.

Today's world, however, is very different. And though we truly like to practice as our ancestors did, it usually isn't possible. There's just no good place in the city to cast a nine-foot circle. But even if there were, athame-waving is against the law. Bonfire-building is considered arson. And since clothing isn't optional, dancing naked in the streets isn't just frowned upon—it's likely to get you arrested.

I have to admit that "practice adjustment" issues didn't concern me much until recently. Why? Because if I needed a wooded area for a ritual, I simply made a phone call. Since most of my friends owned woodland properties, they were happy to help. It just wasn't a problem. It took a move to Maryland to bring things to light. In an area where apartments and condos are the standard dwelling mode, practicing outdoors was simply out of the question. Once I began to see things for what they really were, though, I not only adjusted, but learned some really neat tricks along the way. To that end, I pass them along to you. Use them, expand upon them, and stretch them to the fullest. In doing so, you'll find that urban living doesn't have to present a downside at all. In fact, it can set more magic afoot than any forest glade on the planet.

Helpful Hints

Surround yourself with plants and stones. Their energy not only reinforces your magic, but offers the same magical vibrations found in woodland areas.

Want a magical herb garden? Try a multi-leveled strawberry pot. Plant moisture-loving varieties at the bottom, and reserve the upper areas for those which require good drainage. Don't forget to plant something in the top of the pot. (Miniature roses not only add a festive touch, but also imbue the whole area with love and harmony—and no one can have too much of that!)

While a large space for your circle-casting is nice, it simply isn't necessary. Just expand the circle in your mind—through walls, floors, buildings, etc.—until it meets the necessary dimensions.

Use modern conveniences for all your magical work. Dry herbs on a paper towel in the microwave (check them every five seconds), and chop or powder them with a food processor or blender. Try an electric potpourri pot for making magical oils, and use the drip coffee-maker for infusions, potions, and washes. Don't discount the power of your freezer, either. Just twenty-four hours is all it takes to clear negative energy from magical tools, trinkets, and stones.

Need to toss something into a large body of running water? Just flush it down the toilet or garbage disposal. The only exceptions are large objects, stones, and other rigid materials. Soak those in water overnight, then bury them in a potted plant.

Use the barbecue grill to contain your ritual fire. Because it's designed to withstand heat, it's perfect for burning anything that a candle flame can't handle—even a small Yule log.

Enforce spells by adding a few drops of appropriately scented oil to your central air filters and/or light bulbs. This not only adds power to the spell, but keeps it working indefinitely.

Because city driving can be nerve-wracking, time-consuming, and expensive, don't drive to the store every time you need an appropriately colored candle. Keep a good supply of wide-tipped colored markers and white utility candles, instead. Just use the marker to color the outer candle surface, and you're back to the business at hand.

Magical practice in the city doesn't have to be any more difficult than magical practice anywhere else. It's all a matter of personal creativity—that same strong, wonderful force that has always been the basis for magic. And no matter who we are, or where we live, that's something that we'll never run short of!

For Further Reading
Natural Magick: Inside the Well-Stocked Witch's Cupboard by Sally Dubats.
    Kensington Publishing, 1999.

Magical Connections
by Wren Walker

The old fashioned witch-hunt is definitely a thing of the past. For one thing, a traditional witch-hunt was slow work. Witches, as elusive and provocative as the folktales that they inspired, were often quite hard to find.

Witches had learned from past experience (which we won't dwell on here) how to keep a low profile. They lived in places called "broom closets." If you didn't know someone who knew the Witches, chances were good that you would never get to know them yourself. Like that fleeting glimpse of something seen only from the corner of your eye, Witches hid somewhere between the ethereal plane of magic and the harsh reality of public intolerance.

Anytime a witch-hunter would inquire, "Anyone around here know where I can find some Witches?" —Well, let's just say that things tended to get awfully quiet. Finding Witches the old-fashioned way in the 1970s and '80s was no romp in the rosemary. Many of the witch-hunters finally gave up trying to find the real Witches and just went out and bought a ouija board instead.

Today, one may still hear about a "witch-hunt" as part of a political spin campaign. Sometimes a whistleblower will get fired for reasons drummed up in a "witch-hunt," too. But for all practical purposes, an old-fashioned "witch-hunt" is not likely to ferret out many modern Witches.

For that, one has to do a "search."

Witch Hunting

Just one computer search for the word "Witch" will bring up over 484,000 entries; "Pagan" gets 347,500; and the word "Wicca" will yield 63,000 returns. Even after screening out the references to movies and other unrelated topics, that adds up to a whole lot of Witches, Wiccans, and Pagans out there on the World Wide Web. Where did they all come from?

Working in shops and stores, typing letters in offices, studying in the library, and planning what to make for dinner, Witches, Wiccans, and Pagans are right where they always have been. They are preparing altars, gathering herbs, grinding powders for incense, and setting up the quarter candles for the next Full Moon ritual just as they always have. One thing has changed however: Witches, Wiccans, and Pagans are now on the Internet . . . and they are definitely not hiding anymore!

There are thousands of Pagan message boards, Wiccan chat rooms, and Witch websites. Looking for information about Pagan beliefs? There are web sites devoted to everything from Asatru and Druidism to Christian Witchery and traditional Wicca.

Need to know about your legal rights as a practicing Pagan? There are numerous Pagan educational and anti-discrimination organizations online. Sites like the Alternative Religion Educational Network, the Witches League for Public Awareness, and the Lady Liberty League all feature legal resources and can even provide contact information for legal aid.

Want to chat with Witches, Wiccans, or Pagans? There are e-lists and e-groups, message boards, and chat rooms by the hundreds. Want to meet other Pagans? The Witches' Voice and other networking sites feature on-line state-by-state directories of individual Pagans and groups, upcoming events, festivals, study-groups, and workshops.

Need to find that perfect pentacle for a friend's birthday or a hearthwarming gift for the newly handfasted couple? The Pagan shopping available on the Internet is the busy Kitchen Witch's dream come true!

And let's not forget that all-important gift from the gods: e-mail! Okay, it's true that some of us have a love/hate relationship with our email in-box, but for keeping in touch with Pagan friends or for forwarding the latest news of interest to our fellow Witches, it's still the best invention since candle-wax remover!

Pagans Travel into Cyberspace

At first glance, it might seem to be a rather odd combination: Earth-based religionists and something as ethereal as the Internet. Instead of green rolling hills, a trip to a Pagan website might feature scrolling green Helvetica fonts. The glow of a computer screen certainly can never rival the sheer magic of a late October full Harvest Moon, and yet, there is some undeniable force that draws Pagans into cyberspace with a pull just as strong as the pull our own dear lunar orb exerts upon the tides. Indeed, upon further reflection, it becomes clear that Pagans and Cyberspace are a match designed by the gods themselves.

Pagans understand nature. Our beliefs are based upon seasonal transformations, heavenly circuits, and natural earth rhythms. And if there is any one thing that Pagans understand better than perhaps any other people, it is that everything changes. Change is a function of nature. This is an integral necessity in the circles and cycles of life itself. Change is not at all a frightening concept in Pagan belief systems, so when the Internet technology was born, we quite naturally looked the "new baby" over and almost immediately embraced her with welcome typing fingers.

Pagans are fiercely independent and individualistic in temperament, and we generally look upon these traits with a certain amount of pride. Yet living in a society which still largely mistrusts and misunderstands our belief systems and religions, being a "lone wolf" or even a member of a vital, but isolated, group has its drawbacks. Lacking a larger support system, many individual Pagans or groups had no real idea where other Pagan groups might be, or whether there would be anyone who could aid them if trouble came loping over the next hillside. This trepidation kept many a broom closet fully occupied for decades.

The Internet crosses that psychic divide between the intense desire to remain autonomous to

oneself (or true to one's own tradition) and the equally real necessity of banding together with others in a show of strength and support. As challenges arise, the message spreads swiftly across what has become known as the "Pagan Net."

Magical Connections

Literally within minutes, at least ten Pagans have received the message . . . who pass it on to ten more . . . who then post it on the Pagan message boards . . . and forward it on to the organizations with legal contacts or information . . . who then respond with resources, referrals, advice, and other needed assistance. Within hours, thousands of various and sundry Witches, Wiccans, and Pagans are working together on problem solving, mainstream news media "Wicca 101" education, or inter–pagan coalition building.

The best element in utilizing this sort of model is that once the challenge has been met—and usually it is met quite successfully, I might add!—we various and sundry Witches, Wiccans, and Pagans can all go back to our own autonomous covens and groups, back to our solitary ways, or back to our personal practices until we need to band together once again.

It is the perfect model for Pagans. It is probably the only model that would work for Pagans. No one person or one group is ever "in charge." Project or team leaders may arise because of their skills or networking contacts in any one situation, but it is understood that this leadership spot is to be only a temporary position. (And we'll be sure to remind them of that fact if they seem to forget!)

Through the Internet, Pagans have found covens and groups, formed organizations, met romantic partners, and discussed the news of the day. We have come together to educate the public and dispel the myths surrounding Paganism and Witchcraft. We have provided links to legal resources, raised funds for Pagans who have special or emergency needs, rallied against discrimination, and made great inroads in interfaith communications.

We have shared with each other, grown to know each other, and somewhere along the way we have come to understand each other just a little bit better. We will probably never all agree on everything, and we don't have to. As long as we know that "out there"—somewhere in the vast search engines of the World Wide Web—there are millions of other people who also call themselves "Pagan," we understand that at some level, we are all connected. Those connections remain with us—within us—even when we turn off the computer screen. So log off now, Pagans, and go out dancing, safe and secure, under the light of the mysterious Moon.

Web Addresses
The Witches' Voice at www.witchvox.com
The Witches League for Public Awareness at www.CelticCrow.com
The Alternative Religion Educational Network at aren.org
Lady Liberty League at www.circlesanctuary.org/liberty/

Handfasting
by Jami Shoemaker

A bride in white, vows spoken, rings exchanged, a kiss to seal their love. A hasty exit under a shower of rice. Feasting and merriment, cake and wine. A bouquet thrown to unwed maidens, a garter tossed to unwed men. A secret getaway, a honeymoon filled with lovemaking. The makings of a typical modern wedding? Yes. And the makings of a typical Pagan wedding as well. Like many ceremonies, customs, and traditions today, the typical wedding has its roots in folklore and pagan customs. The modern Pagan or Wiccan handfasting offers an opportunity to reclaim all these familiar customs and more.

History

Handfastings predate modern weddings, and were often performed to seal a couple's commitment to each other in lieu of a legally binding ceremony. A handfasting was originally a betrothal or engagement—a commitment lasting a year and a day. After this "trial run," the couple could choose to remain together and perform a more binding ceremony, or go their separate ways without animosity or obligation. Many Pagans and Wiccans are choosing the ceremony of handfasting as a legally binding rite of their long-term commitment to each other, not "'til death do us part," but "for so long as love endures."

It is important to note that, though most of the customs here imply a heterosexual couple by using the terms "bride" and "groom," a handfasting may be performed for a heterosexual, gay, lesbian, or bisexual couple (or even a polyamorous group.) Regardless, their union reflects the Sacred Marriage of the gods, and is a celebration of love and proclamation of commitment to each other.

Customs and Their Meanings

Handfasting, as the name implies, is literally the tying together of the couple's hands, symbolizing their union. The expression "tying the knot" stems from this old tradition of binding the couple's hands together (right to right and left to left, forming a figure eight or sign of eternity) with a cord during the ceremony.

June has long been the most popular month for weddings. As Beltane, or May Day, celebrated the sacred marriage of the God and Goddess, the entire month of May was devoted to the gods, and it was once forbidden to wed during this time. It seems natural that after the lusty month of May, eager couples would wed as soon as possible. June is named after Juno, the Roman goddess of birth, maidens, mothers, and marriage. June is also the month of the Mead Moon, named after that sweet drink of fermented honey. "Honeymoon" comes from the tradition of marrying in June, and celebrating the event by sharing a drink of mead every day for a month, under the "honey" Moon. Many Pagans also choose to handfast at Imbolc or the equinox, tapping the energies of spring, or at Lughnasadh, enjoying the abundance of the first harvest.

On that special day, the bride represents the Goddess and the groom represents the Lord of the Greenwood. It is interesting that historically, the traditional white gown did not necessarily symbolize the bride's virginity, but rather her association with the maiden aspect of the Triple Goddess.

The ring itself, a perfect circle, represents the Goddess, the wheel of the year and cycle of life, and the never-ending love the couple shares. Placing it on the fourth finger of the left hand positions it over an artery, once believed to run directly from the hand to the heart.

Showering the newlywed couple with rice, grains, or seeds symbolically transfers the fertility of the crop to the couple, as well as ensuring that they will never hunger. Once, wheat biscuits were broken over the bride's head to ensure her fertility. Later, guests piled up small cakes, and if the bride and groom kissed over the top of them without disturbing the cakes, they were guaranteed many children. In today's ceremony, the groom places his hand over the bride's and, together, they plunge the knife into the cake. This act is a reflection of the Great Rite itself, and the sharing of this cake with guests passes the magical energy of the couple and the sweetness of their love to all.

Flowers and herbs, potent with magical meaning, have always been an essential part of any marriage ceremony. Red roses for love, orange blossoms for happiness and fertility, ivy for fidelity, rosemary for remembrance, sage for domestic virtue, and marigolds for sensual passion are just some of the traditional flowers and herbs used in wreaths, bouquets, and floral decorations. The strong scent of herbs (or sometimes garlic) carried by bridesmaids was thought to drive mischievous spirits away, therefore protecting the bride. The bride's bouquet traditionally included myrtle for luck and love. By giving myrtle to her bridesmaids, or tossing her bouquet to the unwed maidens, the bride shares her good fortune. Once, any item worn by a happy bride was considered good luck, and flowers, ribbons, gloves, and stockings were all fair game!

Once made of buckled leather, the garter has long been associated with both weddings and Witches. Among Witches, the garter was worn (and still is in Gardnerian traditions) by the priestess of the coven. A mark of her rank, a buckle was added for each new coven that grew from the original one. In some traditions, only a maiden could be priestess and the garter may have originally been passed, not to the bachelors, but to the next maiden who would take the priestess's place. Later stripped of its spiritual meaning, the garter was simply tossed to guests as a distraction so the couple could slip away. How delightful it would be to keep the gesture, and restore the spiritual power of the garter. Indeed, the garter worn by a priestess and caught by a young man would surely be a gift from the Goddess and a blessing on his manhood!

Another custom that has found its way into modern Pagan handfastings is jumping over a broomstick, which has roots in both African and European tradition. Denied legal marriages, African-American slaves would jump over a broom to seal their vows, or cross two sticks, symbolizing the strength of their commitment. A European twist on this custom is the crossing of a broom and a sword over which the couple jumps, symbolizing the cutting and sweeping away of parental ties. The broom is also a symbol of fertility—the stick representing the male and the broom, the female.

The Ceremony

Although there are many Wiccan and Pagan traditions, each with their own brand of handfasting, some common elements exist. A typical handfasting ceremony will

begin with the casting of a circle, placing the couple and all who attend in a sacred space. The four directions are acknowledged and elementals are invited to join. A priest, priestess, or both may preside over the ceremony. Goddess and God are invoked to bless the bride and groom, whose union reflects the sacred union of the divine. Vows are spoken (many couples write their own, or draw passages from poetry or literature), rings or other tokens are blessed and exchanged, and the couple's hands are bound together. The couple shares drink and/or food, and the marriage is pronounced. Thanks are given to all beings present, the couple shares a kiss and jumps the broom. Feasting, merriment, and gift-giving follow. That night, the sacred union of the God and Goddess is celebrated, as it has been since time immemorial, by yet another happy couple.

For Further Reading

Alternative Weddings: An Essential Guide for Creating Your Own Ceremonies by Jane Ross-MacDonald. Taylor, 1997.

The Alternative Wedding Book (Alternatives for Simple Living Series). Northstone, 1997.

Lunar Spellworking
by Estelle Daniels

Most books on magic say that you should time your spells with the Moon. But what does that mean, exactly? The easiest way is to check what sign the Moon occupies, and then work whichever spells and magic are most favorable under that particular Moon sign.

Now, if you absolutely have to do a love spell today, and the Moon is not in one of the three signs best for love spells (Taurus, Leo, or Libra) you can still do your love spell. But realize that you will have to put a bit more energy and concentration into your spell to make it as effective as if it took place under a more favorable Moon sign.

For this type of astrology, all that matters is the sign the Moon occupies. An astrological almanac will show the date and time when the Moon goes into each sign. That lunar influence is in effect until the Moon goes into the next sign, usually about two-and-a-half days later. There are other factors you can take into account, such as the placement of Venus, Mars, and the Sun, but the Moon is one of the strongest and most immediate astrological factors in spellworking.

Each sign rules many things. If you can find the sign that fits most closely with what you want to accomplish, you get the best results. Each sign is also ruled by one or two planets. If you need the energies of a certain planet, use a sign that it rules. For example, if you want to consecrate an athame, remember that sharp cutting instruments come under Mars' rulership. Mars rules the signs of Aries and Scorpio. Either of those signs would be good, but Scorpio is naturally an occult sign, so Scorpio would be better than Aries for consecrating a magical knife.

Virgo is also good for consecrating an athame, for Virgo is the sign of tools and the tangible effects they have. You have to consider all the factors involved and decide which energies you want. If you use a certain Moon sign, you are tapping into certain specific energies, but also all the energies of that sign in general.

Elements

Each sign has the characteristics of one of the four elements: fire, earth, air, and water. The element of a sign can affect how your spells work.

Fire signs Aries, Leo, and Sagittarius are energetic, rash, sometimes compulsive, and passionate and open. They have faith and zeal. They are forward-looking, and can have a tendency to forget the past in their eagerness to get on with the future.

Earth signs Taurus, Virgo, and Capricorn are stable, immobile, strong and silent, enduring, and practical. They live in the real world, the here and now. They have patience and endurance. They are rooted solidly in the present, make careful long-term plans, and don't like to change the way things were done in the past.

Air signs Gemini, Libra, and Aquarius are very mobile, changeable, and even sometimes fickle. They love to communicate and interact with others, and are very intellectually oriented. They are full of ideas and plans, but sometimes they can be scattered and uncoordinated. They have intelligence and inspiration.

Water signs Cancer, Scorpio, and Pisces are empathic, persistent, and mystical. They are associated with the qualities of remembering, consolidating, quietness, and privacy. They have depth and emotionality. They look to the past, to decide what to do in the present and future. Water rules magic and spells in general, so water signs are often a good choice when you are uncertain as to which sign you should use in your magical work.

Qualities

In addition to an element, each sign also has a quality: cardinal, fixed, or mutable. The quality of the sign can also affect your spells.

Cardinal signs Aries, Cancer, Libra, and Capricorn have active temperaments. They are ambitious, changeable, initiatory, progressive, organizing, independent, and goal-oriented.

Fixed signs Taurus, Leo, Scorpio, and Aquarius have set or solid temperaments. They are dogmatic, unyielding, stubborn, accumulative, dignified, grounded, and steady.

Mutable signs Gemini, Virgo, Sagittarius, and Pisces have changeable or harmonious temperaments. They are versatile, intuitive, diplomatic, sympathetic, and adaptable.

Spell Correspondences

Each sign has been identified with many things and activities which naturally correspond to the energies of that sign. They are traditionally recognized as having certain attributes, and this spell list has been generated using those traditional attributes of each sign.

You may find some things are listed under more than one Moon sign. Many signs overlap somewhat in their rulerships and attributes. Even when the same traits are listed, however, they are slightly altered by the quality and element of their sign—cardinal conflict can be very different from fixed conflict, for example. This gives you a choice of Moons for your spellworking, with subtle differences distinguishing each that can greatly increase the effectiveness of your spells.

Moon in Aries

Spells for health and vitality, and energy workings fall under Aries. Consecrating athames or swords, and working on magical weapons are good choices for this sign. Spells involving conflict, combat, battles, war, warriors, and soldiers are also effective.

Aries rules beginnings, new ventures, and pioneering. Conflict, energy, ego, self, weapons, guns, knives, sharp things, and surgery also fall under this sign. Aries is associated with impatience, sarcasm, quick results, making trouble, rescuing people in trouble, heroism, naiveté, restlessness, and courage.

Moon in Taurus

Spells for prosperity, security, love, music and the arts, business, possessions, self-esteem, values, and ethics work well under this sign. Taurus also rules bindings, strength, endurance, and patience. An earth sign, Taurus is associated with fertility, the essence of the Earth, Gaia, consecrating a pentacle, planting and farming in general, and contacting the Goddess.

This is the sign in which the Moon is strongest and most effective for spellwork, especially at the Full Moon.

Taurus rules anything to do with money, sensuality, dance, and silence. Earth matters, including wealth, greed, and conservation, are affected by this sign. Taurus is soothing and solid, reliable and unshockable. It is also associated with physical love, and is helpful in matters involving sex.

Moon in Gemini
Spells for memory, intelligence, ideas, travel, cars, and transportation in general work well under this sign. Gemini rules buying and selling and commerce, siblings, writing, teaching and learning, computers, communication, and networking. It's a good sign for tool consecration—especially wands, cards, and pictures—gay, bisexual, or transgender issues, and contacting the Goddess.

Gemini rules communication and transportation: Words, cars, and telephones. It also rules things of a dual nature, and is associated with sleight-of-hand, thievery, and mysteries, along with gossip and innuendo. Short trips and field trips, movement, and travel all fall under Gemini, as well as long-distance communication and connections with neighbors and friends.

Moon in Cancer
Spells for home, mothers, family, children, and food are effective under a Cancer Moon. A water sign, Cancer also rules psychic abilities, and divination, past lives, and contacting the Goddess. Spells involving real estate, finding or buying a home, weather workings, planting, and raising food crops also work well under Cancer. This Moon is good for altar consecration, chalice consecration, establishing a covenstead, initiation, and starting a tradition. This is the sign the Moon rules, and here she is very strong.

Cancer is a nurturing sign, and rules security, traditions, cooking and eating, home and hearth, and the family in general. Myths and archetypes, looking into the past, and traditions are associated with

this sign, and it is also good for listening to others, helping with problems, keeping secrets, and doing things at home or for the home.

Moon in Leo
Spells for love, romance and dating, children, creativity, fun, self-expression, play, vacation, and leisure work well under this Moon sign. Investments, speculation, and selling a home at a good profit are also ruled by Leo. As the sign of royalty and pride, Leo governs queens and kings, aristocracy, and awards and recognition.

Leo rules play, parties and fun, celebrations, hobbies, games, and gambling. A spell for naming a child can work particularly well under this Moon. Leo rules love and lovers, loyalty, giving and receiving, chivalry, and warmth.

Moon in Virgo
Spells for health, healing, wellness, herb lore, and medicine are strong under this Moon sign. Study, organizing, business and trade, bureaucracy, logic, analysis, and science are also found under Virgo. Spells for tool consecration in general, and the pentacle in particular, are effective during this Moon. Spells involving coworkers, soldiers and the military, and police and law enforcement also work well.

Virgo rules food and nutrition, herbs, and vitamins. The plastic arts, crafts, pottery, tools, and detail work also fall under Virgo's influence. This sign governs work and the workplace, relationships with relatives and coworkers, obligations, and the needs of the community. It's also a good sign for low magic work, evocations, and coven workings.

Moon in Libra
Spells for legal matters in general, justice, contracts, war and peace, and balance fall under Libra. As the sign of partnerships, Libra will lend energy to spells for love, romance and dating, marriage, beauty and harmony, and music. As the sign of balance, Libra oversees spells for legal matters, lawyers, accountants, team-building, and diplomacy. A Libra Moon also aids spells for other people.

Libra rules balance, diplomacy, negotiation, debate and discussion, politeness, etiquette and manners, and socializing. Libra's dark side can include laziness, tyranny over the weak, and scams, but it can also aid balance in relationships, mentoring, and working with other people.

Moon in Scorpio
Spells for sex, death, initiation, transformation, regeneration, and renewal fall under Scorpio. It is also a good Moon for consecrating an athame or any tool which holds power, and for banishing, forging a group identity, keeping secrets, doing research, uncovering hidden or lost things, developing psychic talents, strengthening the will and willpower, and working magic in general. Divination, contacting other planes, and contacting the dead are also more effective under a Scorpio Moon. Spells involving morals and morality, purgings and purification through suffering, exorcism, hypnotism, energy workings, warriors, and fighters work well under this Moon, too. But remember, this is the sign when the Moon is weakest and least effective.

Scorpio rules merging with another, emotional truths, hidden talents, ritual magic, taboos, and transformative experiences. This sign also rules death and rebirth, transformation, intensity, solitude, solo workings, and workings with two people. Scorpio can govern noble motivations, but it also rules sneaky tactics. It is a sign of extremes, crises, integrity, and mastery.

Moon in Sagittarius
Spells for legal matters in general, laws, judges, teaching and learning, education, philosophy, and ethics work best under the Sagittarius Moon. Spells for dreams, contacting the higher planes, accessing the Akashic records, contacting Deity, divination, and starting a tradition are also effective under this sign. Sagittarius also handles spells for big business, monopolies, publishers and publishing, luck in general, and especially good luck.

Sagittarius rules long journeys, dreamwork, high mysteries, and faith. It is the sign of parties and fun, fame, generosity, wild abandon, serendipity, eternal optimism, and resilience. Sagittarius also rules higher learning, mind expansion, the ability to perceive right and wrong, languages, and thoughts about the future.

Moon in Capricorn

Spells for career, job, business, work, honor and reputation, big business, achievement, awards and recognition, authority in general, world leaders, statesmen, presidents, and government in general work effectively under the Capricorn Moon. But it also the sign where the Moon is weak and operating at a disadvantage.

Capricorn rules professions, inherited traits, responsibility, the public eye, promotion, social standing, degrees and advancement, and employers. An earth sign, Capricorn governs physical manifestations of earth such as mountains, rocks, and stones, and spiritual manifestations such as hard work, social climbing, time and clocks, and ruthlessness. It also the sign of conscience, profound wisdom, the Crone, long-term results, and respect.

Moon in Aquarius

Spells for friends, acquaintances, clubs and organizations, founding a coven, covens in general, and legislative bodies work under the social sign of Aquarius. Spells for hopes, idealism, making the world a better place, utopia, freedom, genius, logic, and luck in general flourish under the auspices of this Moon.

Aquarius rules surprises, circumstances beyond your control, and the future. A "transpersonal" sign, Aquarius is involved in causes, social awareness, astrology, anarchy, social upheaval, and bettering the human condition. Aquarius puts sparks into energy and energy work, meeting new people, and working with a coven. It is also the sign of honesty, nonemotional and objective judgment, trustworthiness, fairness, reason, and aspirations.

Moon in Pisces

Spells for increasing psychic ability, contacting other planes, merging with Deity, and spirituality gain strength under this Moon. Pisces rules the undercurrents of society, so spells involving prisons and prisoners, confinement, the downtrodden and unfortunate, criminals, and hidden enemies work well in this sign. Spells for past lives and karma, reincarnation, magic in general, potions, brews, drawing out poisons, cleansings, secrets and hidden things, and finding lost items are powerful during this time. Pisces also lends power to spells for banishment, exorcism, mediumship, examining the hidden aspects of yourself, and hypnotism. Another "transpersonal" sign, Pisces is good for spells affecting charity and welfare, widows and orphans, psychic healing, working with oils and incenses, luck in general, and bad luck.

Pisces rules escapism, banality, solitude, possession, secret societies, merging with God and Goddess, alcohol, chemicals in general, drugs, potions, and elixirs. Pisces lends energy to facing the past, listening to the still small voice, charity, humanitarian concerns, faith, secrets, and vulnerability. It is a sign for high magic, divine madness, aloneness, ending, and conquering fears.

For Further Reading
The House Book: The Influence of the Planets in the Houses by Stephanie Camilleri. Llewellyn, 1999.
Keywords for Astrology by Hajo Banzhaf and Anna Haebler. Weiser, 1996.
The Rulership Book by Rex E. Bills. American Federation of Astrologers, 1992.

Gingerbread
A Witch's Love Story
by Thea Bloom

I was lustfully eyeballing a collection of eighteenth-century horn hunter's buttons at the Craft and Folk Art Museum in Los Angeles last fall, when I heard someone give me the strangest command. Yes, my brain was telling me, you heard right—that big intimidating security guard in the other room has just barked out, "Hey you—yeah you!—come over here, and smell this case!"

She had twenty pounds and a few inches on me, so I made it snappy through the deserted galleries of the Slovenian exhibit to do what she asked. The case she was referring to was filled with *bosmans*— beautifully intricate hearts made of baked dough.

She pressed her nose into a seam of the glass case and impatiently waved her hand, signaling me to do the same on the other side. "Oh God, Thea," I thought. "Do it for the gipper—just get this over with quickly, politely ingest a nose full of Windex, and you will be back to ogling buttons in no time." I inhaled—and was totally shocked to receive a heavy-duty hit of ginger. I'm talking really good ginger. My fear left me, I raised my eyebrows, I nodded my head; the security guard raised her eyebrows, nodded her head. I sniffed again and smiled, she sniffed again and smiled. I can't tell you how long we both stood at either corner of the case sniffing, smiling and nodding at each other like complete idiots . . . like drug addicts. Did she know I was an aromatherapist? Was she an aromatherapist? Did she ask everyone to do this, or did I just have "bizarre fellow case-sniffer" written all over me? I will never know. But I am grateful to her, for thus began my obsession with the root.

From Slovenia with Love

Rural Slovenians were mad for ginger long before I was, though. They have used gingerbread, or honey dough as they refer to it, to celebrate

the sacredness of the harvest and mark the cornerstones in the lives of the people of their villages from Pagan times through the present. *Botrinas*, or flat breads made from plaited dough braids, are traditionally presented to newborns by their godparents. The bosmans I encountered in the fragrant case were actually traditional wedding breads, either made by hand or pressed from wooden molds to form infants, goddess figures, or hearts. In Pagan times these breads were ritually placed in the bride's lap before she and her groom went to their marriage bed. The Koroska region of Slovenia is known for a wheel-shaped wedding bread known as *podirijanca*. It was named after the symbolic hole in its center and ornamented with dried fruit and cigars. Yeah, you could use plenty of good old-fashioned sexual symbolism in your breads before those Christians came along. Actually, the podirijanca was meant to be thrown into a throng of rowdy wedding guests. A tussle would then ensue, much like the shameless women-knocking-women-to-the-ground kind of battle for the bridal bouquet here in the States today. I tell you, I never did fight for a bridal bouquet in my single days, but I would have thrown a mean elbow for a podirijanca. They are works of art.

After that exhibit I went into a massive Slovenian-inspired gingerthon. I had a brief affair with gingerbread cookies that led me straight into the arms of the ultimate siren—the gingerbread house. I was in love. I pulled a Bobby Fisher, a Terence Malick. I dropped out of sight and became a kitchen shut-in. I was buried in fresh ginger dough for all of December, and I have to say it was the first time I really enjoyed the weeks leading up to Christmas.

Seven Reasons Working with Ginger Can Make You a Kitchen Witch Again

1. Ginger Can Have a Positive Effect on the Mind
Aromatherapy gurus like Wanda Sellar have long thought ginger to be warming to the emotions when they go flat and cold (nice for holiday-induced blues). The oil extracted from the root has been know to sharpen the senses and aid the memory (nice for dealing with holiday-induced confusion and forgetfulness). Ginger is known to be "very cheering and indicated for tiredness"—who doesn't need some cheering and relief from exhaustion in December? And finally, ginger root is stimulating, but unlike other energizing upper-types of essential oils, it has a counterbalancing grounding effect. (Information from Sellar's *Dictionary of Essential Oils*, p. 71.)

2. Ginger Is Said to Have Good Effects on the Body
Since the time of ancient Greece folks have used ginger to strengthen and warm the body. A few drops of ginger essential oil in a warm bath will actually raise most people's body temperature. It is also known to raise a few other things, if you know what I mean. It has been used as an aphrodisiac for ages. A note of caution: Don't play around with essential oils without consulting a good book like Sellar's that lists precautions. Essential oils and herbs are for real—they are powerful. They can be skin irritants, and have dangerous counterindications, so always read up on them first.

3. Ginger Is "The Essential Oil of Courage"
The Emperor card in the tarot is a deeply grounded, methodical, logical, and above all courageous archetype. The Emperor card has ginger

written all over it. We look to our inner Emperor when we need to face our fears and order our chaos. I love a ginger bath or fresh ginger and lemon tea when I am scared, overly emotional, and having trouble prioritizing. (Great at Christmas, or every five minutes for mushy, intuitive types like myself.) Speaking of courage, you will be more likely to attempt a gingerbread house if you have the proper backup and visual inspiration. The best book I have come across in my quest for easy instructions is Christa Currie's *Gingerbread Houses*. Currie has lots of good troubleshooting tips—which if I had read and heeded earlier would have prevented some of my maddening early house cave-ins. But in retrospect, those disasters actually were worth it for the stories alone. Keep in mind that

you can buy all-inclusive kits that come with prebaked gingerbread walls, roofs, etc., along with icing mix and bags of candy, for a reasonable $7.99 at most discount stores. If you have kids, or you yourself are suffering from a short attention span and are afraid of making a big mess, this is the way to go. For the even more courage-challenged, there are entirely prefab, already-assembled houses, ready to decorate, at fancy grocery stores as early as November. I know a hip mom who buys a bunch of these houses every year for her kid and his friends to decorate on his birthday. I loved looking at the pictures of last year's event: All these intent kid faces, in the thick of decorating, totally focused, totally unselfconscious, coming up with all these amazing Picasso-like asymmetrically ornamented masterpiece houses.

4. You Will Have Fun Making Gingerbread

Making gingerbread is a creative act that will indulge your personal need to play as it stimulates your five senses. The softer side of you will love the exotic smell of it on the chopping board and baking in the oven, the tart taste of it with a big glass of milk or morning coffee. You, too, could get blissed-out from the texture and color of all the different candies you pick out and use for decorations. And as far as sound goes, wait till you hear the audible squeals of delight people will let out when they receive a beautiful cookie or, God forbid, a whole gingerbread house. No lie! Let me explain.

5. People Are Weirdly Appreciative of a Gingerbread Gift

I was just blown away by people's reactions upon receiving gingerbread. It's as if you gave them one of your kidneys instead of baked goods. I was surprised and delighted that something I made could provoke so

much loving gratitude—even for the things I made that I thought were lame. Why does an edible house or "man" pleasure humans at such a deep cellular level? Who knows? Maybe our primitive minds love something three-dimensional and pretty that we can marvel at—and then metaphorically kill and eat at any time we choose.

6. Playing Metaphysical Martha Stewart Is More Fun Than Playing Plain Ole Martha Stewart

Here's a great way to put some magical tree ornaments with an Old Norse flair. Make a set of square gingerbread cookies and put a small hole near the top of each before baking. When cool, use colored royal icing to paint a different rune on each square, then string and knot a satin ribbon through the hole to make individual tree ornaments. Or you may want to put the runes in order and string them together to make a runic garland. Use your imagination—be insane. I ran out of time this season, but I bolted awake one morning with an absurd plan to construct a serene winter Shinto shrine gingerbread "house" for my Japanophile friend Frank. Ahhh . . . there's always next year.

7. Reconnecting to the Divine During the Holidays Is Very Comforting

There is something alchemical and goddessy about baking any kind of bread. Baking fun bread like gingerbread makes you feel like Vesta, goddess of the hearth—at Disneyland. This past December's Slovenian foray accidentally helped me reclaim my kitchen as a hearth where I could explore my creativity and capacity to give to those I love. Cait Johnson's *Cooking Like A Goddess* is a must-have book right along these lines. Follow her advice and make a kitchen altar. That alone could send you into an estrogen rhapsody and change the holidays for you this year.

A Basic Recipe

I couldn't write this without including a tried-and-true recipe from my friend's grandmother for "Sturdy Gingerbread Men."

I love to use freshly grated ginger and a little fresh grated orange rind, and dark as opposed to light molasses. But I am a flavor-lovin' gal—you may want a subtler, more readily accepted dough, like the one here.

Mix:
1 cup shortening (or margarine)
1 cup sugar
1 cup light molasses
1 tablespoon vinegar
1 beaten egg

Add:
4 cups flour
1 teaspoon salt
1 teaspoon baking soda
1 teaspoon cinnamon
1 teaspoon ginger

Chill till firm. Roll out dough to ¼ to ⅜ of an inch thick. Cut out 10 to 25 ginger men (depending on cookie cutter size). Bake at 375° for 12 to 15 minutes on foil. Decorate with cinnamon red-hots and white icing when cool if desired. Enjoy—and I hope you indulge your desire to smell a museum case, or conduct other seemingly irrational acts that your intuition or a security guard prompts you to perform down the road.

For Further Reading

Gingerbread Houses: A Complete Guide to Baking, Building, and Decorating by Christa Currie. Main Street Books, 1994.

Gingerbread Houses: Baking and Building Memories by Nonnie Cargas. Krause, 1999.

Gingerbread Houses for Kids by Jennifer A. Ericsson, Beth L. Blair (illustrator). White Birch Press, 1998.

December/January

31 Monday
3rd ♋
☽ v/c 8:43 am
☽ enters ♌ 5:09 pm
Color: Lavender

1 Tuesday
3rd ♌
Color: Peach

New Year's Day
Kwanzaa ends
Birthday of Sir James Frazer,
author of *The Golden Bough*

2 Wednesday
3rd ♌
☽ v/c 6:16 am
☽ enters ♍ 6:34 pm
Color: Purple

3 Thursday
3rd ♍
☿ enters ♒ 4:38 pm
Color: Green

Death of Edgar Cayce, psychic

4 Friday
3rd ♍
☽ v/c 2:30 am
☽ enters ♎ 8:23 pm
Color: White

Aquarian Tabernacle Church
registered in Australia by
Lady Tamara Von Forslun, 1994

Set in Eastern Standard Time (EST)

☽ Saturday
3rd ♎
4th Quarter 10:55 pm
Color: Red

*Follow a Twelfth Night tradition in
England by taking mulled cider to a sacred
tree and drinking to its good health*

6 Sunday
4th ♎
☽ v/c 11:05 am
☽ enters ♏ 11:41 pm
Color: Pink

*Twelfth Night/Epiphany
Patricia Crowther's Witchcraft
radio show, A Spell of Witchcraft,
airs in Britain, 1971*

January

7 Monday
4th ♏
Color: Lavender

8 Tuesday
4th ♏
☽ v/c 4:03 pm
Color: White

Death of Dion Fortune, 1946
Birthday of MacGregor Mathers,
one of the three original founders
of the Golden Dawn, 1854

9 Wednesday
4th ♏
☽ enters ♐ 4:57 am
Color: Brown

Jamie Dodge wins lawsuit against
the Salvation Army, which fired her
based on her Wiccan religion, 1989

10 Thursday
4th ♐
Color: Green

11 Friday
4th ♐
☽ v/c 1:49 am
☽ enters ♑ 12:18 pm
Color: Pink

*To wash away illness, according to Gypsy
tradition, cut the person's hair or trim
his fingernails; then throw the clippings
into a body of flowing water*

Set in Eastern Standard Time (EST)

Midwinter Incense

2 parts benzoin
1 part willow wood
1 part crushed rowan berries
½ part periwinkle flowers
½ part lily of the valley flowers

The ratio of herbs to each other is more important in the recipe than the amount (although you should use enough to handle easily). In a bowl or with mortar and pestle, blend the benzoin with the willow wood, then add the crushed rowan berries. Add periwinkle and lily of the valley, mix well.

Self-igniting charcoal blocks are the best way to burn the kinds of incense in this datebook. Blocks can be obtained from most herbal and occult supply stores. Light the block with a match, and place in a dish or fireproof container. Sprinkle the incense on the charcoal block to burn it.

— Anna Franklin

12 Saturday
4th ♑
Color: Gray

Mary Smith hanged in England; she had quarreled with neighbors, who said that the Devil appeared to her as a black man, 1616

☽ Sunday
4th ♑
New Moon 8:29 am
☽ v/c 2:24 pm
☽ enters ♒ 9:41 pm
Color: Gold

Final witchcraft laws repealed in Austria, 1787

Set in Eastern Standard Time (EST)

January

14 Monday
1st ♒
⚶ D 3:45 pm
Color: Silver

Official Confession of Error by
jurors of Salem Witch trials, 1696

Human Be-In, a Pagan-style festival,
takes place in San Francisco, attended by
Timothy Leary and Allen Ginsburg, 1967

15 Tuesday
1st ♒
☽ v/c 7:25 pm
Color: Black

16 Wednesday
1st ♒
☽ enters ♓ 9:00 am
Color: Yellow

Birthday of Dr. Dennis Carpenter,
Circle Sanctuary

17 Thursday
1st ♓
Color: Violet

*Scatter lavender in the bed sheets to provide
comfort and encourage a relaxing night's sleep*

18 Friday
1st ♓
☿ ℞ 3:52 pm
♂ enters ♈ 5:53 pm
☽ v/c 9:27 pm
☽ enters ♈ 9:35 pm
♀ enters ♒ 10:42 pm
Color: Rose

Set in Eastern Standard Time (EST)

Almond Custard

3 cups milk
¼ cup sugar
4 eggs
½ teaspoon vanilla
2 teaspoons almond extract
1 tablespoon finely chopped almonds

Imbolc is traditionally a time to serve milk and dairy dishes. It's one of my favorite excuses to have the oven on for an hour or so in winter.

Mix together all the ingredients, except the chopped almonds, and pour into an ungreased 2-quart baking dish. Sprinkle on the chopped almonds and bake at 325° for 60 minutes, or until a knife inserted comes out clean. Remove from the oven and let cool for a few minutes, then refrigerate. Serves 4 to 6.

— Magenta Griffith

19 Saturday
1st ♈
Color: Indigo

Birthday of Dorothy Clutterbuck, who initiated Gerald Gardner

20 Sunday
1st ♈
☉ enters ♒ 1:02 am
☽ v/c 8:50 pm
Color: Orange

Sun enters Aquarius

Set in Eastern Standard Time (EST)

January

☉ Monday
1st ♈
☽ enters ♉ 9:47 am
2nd Quarter 12:47 pm
Color: White

*Birthday of Martin Luther King, Jr.
(observed)
Celtic Tree Month of Rowan begins*

22 Tuesday
2nd ♉
Color: Gray

*Use lemon in ritual love spells during a waxing
Moon—Venus will value the act due to the
lunar fruit's healing and purifying properties*

23 Wednesday
2nd ♉
☽ v/c 7:29 am
☽ enters ♊ 7:28 pm
Color: White

24 Thursday
2nd ♊
Color: Turquoise

25 Friday
2nd ♊
☽ v/c 2:23 pm
Color: Peach

Birthday of Robert Burns, Scottish poet

Rowan

As our spirits wax with the new year, the Rowan Moon compels us to achieve the inner strength that allows us to triumph over enemies and danger. The rowan has been used for protecting dwellings, barns, and graveyards; to enhance healing and divination rituals; and to increase our own sense of inner power so that we can flow with—never against—the spiral forces of the universe.

Close your eyes and spread your arms, reaching high. Visualize them as branches of the rowan. Imagine that your feet are projecting anchoring roots deep into the center of the earth. Your body is the rowan's trunk. Feel it grow stronger, holding firm against whatever onslaught the elements can produce. Know that with each passing year your trunk grows stronger: A bulwark against anything the universe can hurl at you. Each year it is easier to cope with adversity, easier to turn back ill-will and deflect danger. Know that you are the rowan, sturdy and confident, rooted in Mother Earth while reaching for Father Sky.

— Edain McCoy

26 Saturday
2nd ♊
☽ enters ♋ 1:17 am
☽ v/c 2:03 pm
Color: Blue

Integrate eggs into fertility spell work: they symbolize the womb that holds the origin of life

27 Sunday
2nd ♋
Color: Gold

Set in Eastern Standard Time (EST)

January/February

☽ Monday
2nd ♋
☽ enters ♌ 3:31 am
Full Moon 5:50 pm
Color: Gray

Cold Moon

29 Tuesday
3rd ♌
☽ v/c 6:04 pm
Color: Red

30 Wednesday
3rd ♌
☽ enters ♍ 3:40 am
Color: Brown

Birthday of Zsusanna Budapest, feminist Witch

31 Thursday
3rd ♍
☽ v/c 6:46 am
Color: Violet

Dr. Fian, believed to be the head of the North Berwick Witches, found guilty and executed for witchcraft in Scotland by personal order of King James VI (James I of England), 1591

1 Friday
3rd ♍
☽ enters ♎ 3:44 am
Color: Peach

Set in Eastern Standard Time (EST)

Imbolc

Imbolc is an important day of purification and initiation; on the Sun's day, February 2, the energies are very airy. This Sabbat is a good day for coven work, with an emotionally detached masculine Moon and Sun on the Sun's day.

Dress yourself and your altar in white, while serving white beverages or any dairy food to honor the calving season. Spread the top of a one-pound round of Camembert or Brie cheese with raspberry preserves. Cut a circle of puff pastry large enough to cover the cheese, and wrap it, tucking the ends of the pastry under. Use scraps to decorate the top with Goddess symbols. Brush with beaten egg yolk. Bake at 425° until golden, and serve hot and melting on crackers. During this ritual, bless and dedicate all the candles you will need for other ritual work throughout the year. A good way to start the ceremony is to light candles in the darkened room with chanting to encourage the lengthening days.

— K. D. Spitzer

2 Saturday
3rd ♎
☽ v/c 7:45 pm
Color: Indigo

Imbolc
Groundhog Day
Leo Martello becomes a third-degree Welsh traditionalist, 1973

3 Sunday
3rd ♎
☽ enters ♏ 5:35 am
☿ enters ♑ 11:19 pm
Color: Yellow

Set in Eastern Standard Time (EST)

February

○ Monday
3rd ♏
4th Quarter 8:33 am
Color: Gray

Charge a magical talisman by empowering it with your breath, sleeping with it under your pillow, or placing it in a natural vessel to be enveloped by moonshine

5 Tuesday
4th ♏
☽ v/c 9:02 am
☽ enters ♐ 10:21 am
Color: Black

Imbolc cross-quarter day
(Sun reaches 15° Aquarius)

6 Wednesday
4th ♐
Color: White

7 Thursday
4th ♐
☽ v/c 7:38 am
☽ enters ♑ 6:08 pm
♄ D 8:32 pm
Color: Violet

Death of Thomas Aquinas, scholar who wrote that heresy was a product of ignorance and therefore criminal, and who refuted the *Canon Episcopi*, 1274

8 Friday
4th ♑
☿ D 12:28 pm
♀ enters ♒ 1:39 pm
Color: White

Birthday of Susun Weed, owner of Wise Woman Publishing

Birthday of Evangeline Adams, American astrologer

Set in Eastern Standard Time (EST)

9 Saturday
4th ♑
⚷ enters ♊ 6:19 am
Color: Gray

10 Sunday
4th ♑
☽ v/c 1:50 am
☽ enters ♒ 4:15 am
Color: Orange

Zsusanna Budapest arrested and later
convicted for fortunetelling, 1975

Set in Eastern Standard Time (EST)

February

11 Monday
4th ♒
♀ enters ♓ 8:18 pm
Color: Lavender

☽ Tuesday
4th ♒
New Moon 2:41 am
☽ v/c 5:21 am
☽ enters ♓ 3:53 pm
Color: Red

Chinese New Year (horse)
Mardi Gras
Gerald Gardner, founder of the
Gardnerian tradition, dies
of heart failure, 1964

13 Wednesday
1st ♓
☿ enters ♒ 12:20 pm
Color: Brown

Ash Wednesday

14 Thursday
1st ♓
☽ v/c 2:44 am
Color: Green

Valentine's Day
Elsie Blum, a farmhand from
Oberstedten, Germany, sentenced
to death for witchcraft, 1652

15 Friday
1st ♓
☽ enters ♈ 4:26 am
Color: Pink

Pope Leo X issues bull to ensure that the
secular courts carry out executions of
Witches convicted by the Inquisition,
1521; the bull was a response to the courts'
refusal to carry out the work of the Church

Set in Eastern Standard Time (EST)

Brighid Incense

1 part birch bark
1 part willow bark
1 part oak bark
½ part bistort root
¼ part blackberry leaves
1 part crushed rowan berries
½ part snowdrop flowers
¼ part flax flowers

In a small bowl or with mortar and pestle, crush birch, willow, and oak bark together. Add bistort root and blackberry leaves and mix well. Blend in crushed rowan berries, snowdrop flowers, and flax flowers. Burn on a small charcoal block.

— Anna Franklin

16 Saturday
1st ♈
Color: Blue

17 Sunday
1st ♈
☽ v/c 2:55 pm
☽ enters ♉ 4:58 pm
Color: Yellow

To bring optimism during the dark winter, adorn your home with wreaths of evergreen and decorate with objects representative of spring

Set in Eastern Standard Time (EST)

February

18 Monday
1st ♉
☉ enters ♓ 3:13 pm
Color: Silver

Presidents' Day (observed)
Sun enters Pisces
Celtic Tree Month of Ash begins

19 Tuesday
1st ♉
☽ v/c 6:34 pm
Color: Gray

○ Wednesday
1st ♉
☽ enters ♊ 3:50 am
2nd Quarter 7:02 am
Color: White

Society for Psychical Research,
devoted to paranormal research,
founded in London, 1882

21 Thursday
2nd ♊
Color: Turquoise

Stewart Farrar initiated into
Alexandrian Wicca, 1970
Birthday of Patricia Telesco,
Wiccan author
Death of Theodore Parker Mills,
Wiccan elder, 1996

22 Friday
2nd ♊
☽ v/c 2:53 am
♀ enters ♓ 5:27 am
☽ enters ♋ 11:16 am
Color: Peach

Birthday of Sibyl Leek, Wiccan author
Birthday of ShadowCat, Wiccan author

Set in Eastern Standard Time (EST)

Ash

The Ash Moon is the balancing force that connects all of us with all worlds, seen and unseen. It offers potent energy for healing spells, psychic work, protection in or on water, dream magic, and curse-breaking.

For this ritual you will need an ash limb, or you may wish to decorate and empower a dowel as an ash substitute. Face each direction in turn—moving clockwise and starting in the west—while holding the ash wand before you. Visualize it beating down any curse energy or ill-will being sent your way.

> *By the ash to all worlds my will does go,*
> *To those who would curse, I say them, "No!"*
> *The ash protects and absorbs the bane,*
> *Breaking the curse so I'm whole again.*

End the ritual by taking the wand outside and placing it on the ground so the negativity will be grounded.

— Edain McCoy

23 Saturday
2nd ♋
Color: Brown

24 Sunday
2nd ♋
☽ v/c 8:39 am
☽ enters ♌ 2:36 pm
Color: Gold

To bring good luck, use violets as a charm ingredient in a talisman or amulet; ask Aphrodite to bless her sacred flower

Set in Eastern Standard Time (EST)

February/March

25 Monday
2nd ♌
Color: White

26 Tuesday
2nd ♌
☽ v/c 11:30 am
☽ enters ♍ 2:47 pm
Color: Black

Purim

☺ Wednesday
2nd ♍
Full Moon 4:17 am
☽ v/c 10:17 pm
Color: Peach

Quickening Moon
Pope John XXII issues first bull to discuss the practice of witchcraft, 1318
Birthday of Rudolph Steiner, philosopher and father of the biodynamic farming movement

28 Thursday
3rd ♍
☽ enters ♎ 1:47 pm
Color: Violet

1 Friday
3rd ♎
♂ enters ♉ 10:05 am
♃ D 10:15 am
Color: Peach

Birthday of the Golden Dawn, 1888
Covenant of the Goddess (COG) formed, 1975
Preliminary hearings in the Salem Witch trials held, 1692

Set in Eastern Standard Time (EST)

2 Saturday
3rd ♎
☽ v/c 6:57 am
☽ enters ♏ 1:51 pm
Color: Gray

When you are a recipient of honors, do as the Romans did—hang a laurel wreath on the door as a sign of victory

3 Sunday
3rd ♏
Color: Yellow

March

4 Monday
3rd ♏
☽ v/c 9:43 am
☽ enters ♐ 4:55 pm
Color: Lavender

Church of All Worlds incorporates in Missouri, 1968, becoming the first Wiccan church to incorporate in the U.S.

☽ Tuesday
3rd ♐
4th Quarter 8:25 pm
Color: Red

6 Wednesday
4th ♐
☽ v/c 9:31 pm
☽ enters ♑ 11:48 pm
Color: Brown

Birthday of Laurie Cabot, Wiccan author

7 Thursday
4th ♑
♀ enters ♈ 8:42 pm
Color: Green

William Butler Yeats initiated into the Isis-Urania Temple of the Golden Dawn, 1890

8 Friday
4th ♑
☽ v/c 10:06 am
Color: White

Recreate the tradition of Greek brides—place a lump of sugar in your right glove to symbolize the wish for a sweet life

Spring Incense

3 parts frankincense
1 part benzoin
½ part pine resin
½ part bistort
1 part acacia
½ part bluebell flowers
1 part gorse flowers

In a bowl or with mortar and pestle, blend frankincense, benzoin, and pine resin. Add acacia and bistort, mixing thoroughly. Add crushed flowers last. Burn the incense on a small charcoal block.

— Anna Franklin

9 Saturday
4th ♑
☽ enters ♒ 9:56 am
Color: Indigo

10 Sunday
4th ♒
Color: Gold

Dutch clairvoyant and psychic healer Gerard Croiser born, 1909
Date recorded for first meeting of Dr. John Dee and Edward Kelly, 1582

Set in Eastern Standard Time (EST)

March

11 Monday
4th ♒
☽ v/c 2:28 pm
☿ enters ♓ 6:34 pm
☽ enters ♓ 9:56 pm
Color: White

*Burn dragon's blood incense to amplify
your power prior to spell crafting*

12 Tuesday
4th ♓
Color: Black

Stewart Edward White, psychic
researcher, born, 1873; he later
became president of the
American Society for Psychical
Research in San Francisco

☽ Wednesday
4th ♓
New Moon 9:03 pm
☽ v/c 9:03 pm
Color: Yellow

14 Thursday
1st ♓
☽ enters ♈ 10:34 am
Color: Turquoise

Jacques de Molay, head of the
Knights Templar in France, retracts
his confession of heresy before being
burned at the stake, 1314

15 Friday
1st ♈
Color: Rose

Islamic New Year
Pete Pathfinder Davis becomes the first
Wiccan priest elected as president of the
Interfaith Council of Washington State

Set in Eastern Standard Time (EST)

Alder

The Alder Moon brings out our inner psychic. European folklore tells us an alder's energy is eternal, and it should never be cut down. Alder has been used to assist in divination rituals, and wind instruments made of the wood have aided in summoning spirits and working with weather magic. In Celtic mythology the alder is sacred to the god Bran, whose severed head became an oracle.

Open your psychic channels by lying flat on your back. Place a sprig of alder at the top of your head to bridge the path to Bran. Place alder leaves or bark chips on your forehead and near your mouth, and another on your belly to help you have the right "gut reactions" to psychic images.

Ask Bran's assistance, relax completely, and focus on receiving impressions from the Otherworld. Wait to interpret what you see or hear until later. Sleep with some of the alder from your ritual under your pillow to dream prophetically and, perhaps, to clarify your psychic visions.

— Edain McCoy

16 Saturday
1st ♈
☽ v/c 4:08 pm
☽ enters ♉ 11:01 pm
Color: Brown

17 Sunday
1st ♉
Color: Orange

St. Patrick's Day
Eleanor Shaw and Mary Phillips executed in England for bewitching a woman and her two children, 1705

March

18 Monday
1st ♉
Color: Silver

Celtic Tree Month of Alder begins
Birthday of Edgar Cayce,
psychic researcher

19 Tuesday
1st ♉
☽ v/c 7:53 am
☽ enters ♊ 10:20 am
Color: Gray

Elizabethan statute against witchcraft
enacted, 1563; this statute was replaced in
1604 by a stricter one from King James I

20 Wednesday
1st ♊
♇ ℞ 9:55 am
☉ enters ♈ 2:16 pm
Color: Peach

Ostara/Spring Equinox
Sun enters Aries
International Astrology Day

☽ Thursday
1st ♊
☽ v/c 1:14 pm
☽ enters ♋ 7:06 pm
2nd Quarter 9:28 pm
Color: Green

Green Egg Magazine founded, 1968
Inauguration of the Isis-Urania Temple of
the Golden Dawn and initiation of Mina
Bergson (Moina Mathers), 1888
Mandate of Henry VIII against witchcraft
enacted, 1542; repealed in 1547

22 Friday
2nd ♋
Color: White

Pope Clement urged by Phillip IV
to suppress Templar order, 1311

Set in Eastern Standard Time (EST)

Ostara

Ostara or the Spring Equinox brings a waxing Sun. The forces of night are held at bay for the moment, and indeed will continue to give way to the power of the Sun. The Sun enters Aries on March 20, the day of Mercury, and in the hour of the Moon, and begins its circumnavigation of the zodiac. The Moon is skipping ahead of the Sun at 14 degrees Gemini, and Mercury energy dominates this day. Only easily completed projects should be started. Although the Sun and Moon are fire and air, this is a fertility festival and is symbolized by the egg.

Celebrate at sunrise, using pink, pale green, lavender, and butter yellow at the four corners of your altar. Decorate the altar with an egg tree, or search out a pysanki egg with appropriate symbols and nestle it in a bird's nest. Follow with a breakfast brunch; serve eggs!

Create ritual incense for fire and air symbolism. Blend rue, fennel seed, red sandalwood, and cinnamon; add an equal amount of frankincense and several drops of rose oil. Cover and store for two weeks before using.

— K. D. Spitzer

23 Saturday
2nd ♋
☽ v/c 5:19 am
Color: Gray

24 Sunday
2nd ♋
☽ enters ♌ 12:12 am
Color: Yellow

Palm Sunday

Birthday of Alyson Hannigan, who plays Willow on *Buffy the Vampire Slayer*

Arrest of Florence Newton, one of the few Witches burned in Ireland, 1661

March

25 Monday
2nd ♌
☽ v/c 8:57 pm
Color: Lavender

Innocent III issues bull to
establish the Inquisition, 1199

26 Tuesday
2nd ♌
☽ enters ♍ 1:44 am
Color: White

Birthday of Joseph Campbell, author
and professor of mythology

27 Wednesday
2nd ♍
☽ v/c 8:31 pm
⚹ D 10:27 pm
Color: Brown

☺ Thursday
2nd ♍
☽ enters ♎ 1:04 am
Full Moon 1:25 pm
Color: Violet

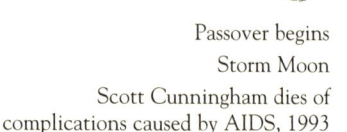

Passover begins
Storm Moon
Scott Cunningham dies of
complications caused by AIDS, 1993

29 Friday
3rd ♎
☿ enters ♈ 9:44 am
☽ v/c 7:57 pm
Color: Pink

Good Friday

Set in Eastern Standard Time (EST)

Spring Salad

1 16-ounce small-curd cottage cheese
½ cup finely minced carrots
½ cup finely minced celery
¼ cup finely minced green pepper
¼ cup finely minced scallions or green onions
1 tablespoon dill

This is a delightful and easy dish; you can add other fresh vegetables that are coming into season. To save time, you may wish to use a food processor to mince the vegetables.

Mix all the ingredients in a bowl, cover and chill. If you want to get fancy, serve on lettuce leaves garnished with a radish rose and green pepper rings. Makes 4 servings

— Magenta Griffith

30 Saturday
3rd ♎
☽ enters ♏ 12:21 am
Color: Blue

31 Sunday
3rd ♏
☽ v/c 9:13 pm
Color: Gold

Easter
Last Witch trial in Ireland,
held at Magee Island, 1711

April

1 Monday
3rd ♏
♀ enters ♉ 1:39 am
☽ enters ♐ 1:48 am
Color: Silver

April Fools' Day

2 Tuesday
3rd ♐
Color: Red

*When the dark wintry days are over,
celebrate spring by hiding decorated eggs,
and serve sacred foods as part of a
ritual feast including fish and sweet breads*

3 Wednesday
3rd ♐
☽ v/c 2:13 am
☽ enters ♑ 6:58 am
Color: Yellow

Passover ends

◯ Thursday
3rd ♑
4th Quarter 10:29 am
Color: Turquoise

5 Friday
4th ♑
☽ v/c 4:59 am
☽ enters ♒ 4:07 pm
Color: Pink

Trial of Alice Samuel, her
husband, and daughter, who
were accused of bewitching the
wife of Sir Henry Cromwell and
several village children, 1593

Set in Eastern Standard Time (EST)

Divination Incense

2 parts white sandalwood
1 part hazel wood
1 part acacia
½ part calendula flowers
½ part bay
½ part clary sage
Pinch of nutmeg

In a bowl or with a mortar and pestle, blend together sandalwood, hazel wood, and acacia. Gradually add calendula flowers, bay, and sage, and stir until well mixed. Drop in nutmeg, and burn on a charcoal block.

— Anna Franklin

6 Saturday
4th ≈
Color: Blue

Integrate patchouli oil into your divination work by sanctifying candles with it

7 Sunday
4th ≈
☽ v/c 11:09 pm
Color: Orange

Daylight Saving Time begins at 2:00 am
Church of All Worlds founded, 1962
First Wiccan "tract" published
by Pete Pathfinder Davis, 1996

Set in Eastern Standard Time (EST)

April

8 Monday
4th ♒
☽ enters ♓ 3:57 am
Color: White

William Alexander Aynton initiated into the Isis–Urania temple of the Golden Dawn, 1896; he would later be called the "Grand Old Man" of the Golden Dawn

9 Tuesday
4th ♓
Color: Gray

10 Wednesday
4th ♓
☽ v/c 12:31 pm
☽ enters ♈ 4:40 pm
Color: Peach

Birthday of Rev. Montague Summers, orthodox scholar and author of *A History of Witchcraft and Demonology*, 1880

11 Thursday
4th ♈
Color: White

Burning of Major Weir, Scottish "sorcerer" who confessed of his own accord, 1670; some historians believe that the major became delusional or senile because up until his confession he had an excellent reputation and was a pillar of society

☽ Friday
4th ♈
New Moon 2:21 pm
Color: Rose

Handfasting of Oberon and Morning Glory Zell, 1974

Set in Eastern Standard Time (EST)

13 Saturday
1st ♈
☽ v/c 4:52 am
☽ enters ♉ 4:55 am
☿ enters ♉ 5:10 am
♂ enters ♊ 12:36 pm
Color: Gray

First confession of witchcraft by Isobel Gowdie, whose case is considered unusual because no torture was used to extract her confession, Scotland, 1662

14 Sunday
1st ♉
Color: Yellow

Adoption of the Principles of Wiccan Belief at "Witch Meet" in St. Paul, Minnesota, 1974

Set in Eastern Standard Time (EST)

April

15 Monday
1st ♉
☽ v/c 11:53 am
☽ enters ♊ 3:56 pm
Color: Lavender

Celtic Tree Month of Willow begins
Birthday of Elizabeth Montgomery, who played Samantha on *Bewitched*

16 Tuesday
1st ♊
Color: White

Birthday of Margot Adler, author of *Drawing Down the Moon*

17 Wednesday
1st ♊
☿ ℞ 1:39 am
☽ v/c 9:17 pm
Color: Brown

Aleister Crowley breaks into and takes over the Golden Dawn temple, providing the catalyst for the demise of the original Golden Dawn, 1900

18 Thursday
1st ♊
☽ enters ♋ 1:01 am
Color: Violet

19 Friday
1st ♋
☽ v/c 6:55 pm
Color: Peach

Conviction of Witches at second of four famous trials at Chelmsford, England, 1579

Set in Eastern Standard Time (EST)

Willow

Like the willow that bends but doesn't break, the Willow Moon helps us do whatever we have to do. It teaches us that we are able to push ourselves to levels we once thought impossible. Once we attain things hard won, the willow offers itself as a glue to bind them to us forever.

Binding must be entered into with care. Because we are all linked on wheel of life, the energies we put in motion will eventually make a full circle and come back to us.

With willow branches, you can bind to yourself any object or idea, or you can bind the actions of someone doing harm. Soak the branches overnight in water containing a few drops of patchouli oil. Take a symbol of the thing to be bound, and wrap it snugly in the branches. Tie it closed until the branches dry. Present the object to the four elements to garner their assistance. When you are finished, keep the object hidden.

— Edain McCoy

○ Saturday
1st ♋
☉ enters ♉ 1:20 am
☽ enters ♌ 7:20 am
2nd Quarter 7:48 am
Color: Brown

Sun enters Taurus

21 Sunday
2nd ♌
Color: Orange

Eat tangerines to enhance your mental prowess before brainstorming sessions at work

April

22 Monday
2nd ♌
☽ v/c 7:30 am
☽ enters ♍ 10:35 am
Color: Gray

Earth Day; the first Earth Day was in 1970

23 Tuesday
2nd ♍
Color: Red

Edward III of England begins the Order of the Garter, which Margaret Murray later links to witchcraft, 1350

First National All-Woman Conference on Women's Spirituality held, Boston, 1976

24 Wednesday
2nd ♍
☽ v/c 9:06 am
☽ enters ♎ 11:22 am
Color: White

25 Thursday
2nd ♎
♀ enters ♊ 12:57 pm
Color: Green

USA *Today* reports that Patricia Hutchins is the first military Wiccan granted religious leave for the sabbats, 1989

☺ Friday
2nd ♎
☽ v/c 8:29 am
☽ enters ♏ 11:15 am
Full Moon 10:00 pm
Color: Rose

Wind Moon

Set in Eastern Standard Time (EST)

Beltane Incense

4 parts frankincense
1 part oak bark
½ part sorrel
1 part hawthorn flowers
½ part primrose flowers
½ part apple blossoms

In a bowl or using a mortar and pestle, mix frankincense with oak bark. Add sorrel, hawthorn, primrose, and apple blossoms and blend well. Burn on a charcoal block.

— Anna Franklin

27 Saturday
3rd ♏
Color: Indigo

A combination of frankincense, rosemary, and sage is an excellent aid to meditation incense

28 Sunday
3rd ♏
☽ v/c 9:25 am
☽ enters ♐ 12:13 pm
Color: Gold

Set in Eastern Standard Time (EST)

April/May

29 Monday
3rd ♐
Color: Silver

Birthday of Ed Fitch, Wiccan author

30 Tuesday
3rd ♐
☿ enters ♊ 2:15 am
☽ v/c 1:10 pm
☽ enters ♑ 4:03 pm
Color: Black

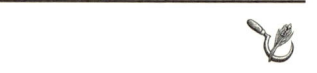

Walpurgis Night; traditionally the German Witches gather on the Blocksberg, a mountain in northeastern Germany

Alex Sanders, founder of the Alexandrian Tradition of witchcraft, dies of lung cancer, 1988

1 Wednesday
3rd ♑
☽ v/c 12:17 pm
Color: Yellow

Beltane/May Day

Order of the Illuminati, an organization dedicated to ceremonial magic, formed in Bavaria by Adam Weishaupt, 1776

Death of Arnold Crowther, stage magician and Gardnerian Witch, 1974

2 Thursday
3rd ♑
☽ enters ♒ 11:43 pm
Color: Green

Steep strawberries with sweet woodruff for a Beltane present

3 Friday
3rd ♒
Color: Peach

Orthodox Good Friday
Birthday of D. J. Conway, Wiccan author

Set in Eastern Standard Time (EST)

Beltane

Prepare for Beltane by leaving tokens for the fairy folk in the woods or in your herb garden. Tie glitzy ribbons for the undines near a natural spring or riverbank. Gather spring flowers at dawn to adorn your door, and prepare a traditional May bowl for your ritual.

First, harvest several stems of flowering sweet woodruff to steep in white wine or champagne. Then stir in a cup of brandy or strawberry wine, adding whole strawberries, rose petals, and floating red candles. Empower the whole bowl for your ritual. Make a mini-Maypole for your altar. Find small smooth egg-shaped stones and half-bury in pots of herbs or directly in the soil to update the ancient tradition of Hermes seeding the soil for fertility. For this ritual, use red as the main color theme in circle as a nod to the red moonflow of ancient ceremonies.

— K. D. Spitzer

○ Saturday
3rd ≈
4th Quarter 2:16 am
Color: Gray

The *New York Herald Tribune* carries the story of a woman who brought her neighbor to court on a charge of bewitchment, 1895

5 Sunday
4th ≈
☽ v/c 7:46 am
☽ enters ♓ 10:46 am
Color: Orange

Orthodox Easter
Cinco de Mayo

Set in Eastern Standard Time (EST)

May

6 Monday
4th ♓
☽ v/c 9:11 pm
Color: Lavender

Beltane cross-quarter day
(Sun reaches 15° Taurus)

Long Island Church of Aphrodite
formed by Reverend Gleb Botkin, 1938

7 Tuesday
4th ♓
☽ enters ♈ 11:22 pm
Color: White

8 Wednesday
4th ♈
Color: Brown

*If someone outside your sacred circle
touches your mojo bag or peers inside it,
reconsecrate it with a purification
ritual and dip it into anointed water*

9 Thursday
4th ♈
Color: Turquoise

Joan of Arc canonized, 1920

First day of the Lemuria, a Roman
festival of the dead; this festival
was probably borrowed from the
Etruscans and is one possible
ancestor of our modern Halloween

10 Friday
4th ♈
☽ v/c 8:47 am
☽ enters ♉ 11:32 am
Color: Pink

Set in Eastern Standard Time (EST)

Macaroon Brownies

⅜ cup (¾ stick) butter or margarine
⅜ cup cocoa
2 eggs
⅛ teaspoon salt
1 cup sugar
1 teaspoon vanilla
½ cup flour
½ cup shredded coconut

Preheat oven to 350° and grease a 8 x 8 pan. Melt butter or margarine in a saucepan. Remove from heat, and add cocoa. Beat eggs and salt until light (about 5 minutes). Gradually add sugar, and then add vanilla. Fold in the chocolate mixture, mixing only until blended. Fold in flour, mixing only until the flour is no longer visible. Add the coconut and stir again— but do not overmix. Pour into the pan, and bake 25–30 minutes.

— Magenta Griffith

11 Saturday
4th ♉
Color: Blue

Massachusetts Bay Colony Puritans
ban Christmas celebrations
because they are too Pagan, 1659

☽ Sunday
4th ♉
New Moon 5:45 am
☽ v/c 7:29 pm
☽ enters ♊ 10:04 pm
Color: Peach

Mother's Day

Set in Eastern Standard Time (EST)

May

13 Monday
1st ♊
♆ ℞ 7:10 am
Color: Silver

Celtic Tree Month of Hawthorn begins

14 Tuesday
1st ♊
⚷ enters ♋ 1:22 am
♀ enters ♈ 8:16 am
Color: Black

Widow Robinson of Kidderminster
and her two daughters are arrested for
trying to prevent the return of Charles II
from exile by use of magic, 1660

15 Wednesday
1st ♊
☽ v/c 4:08 am
☽ enters ♋ 6:33 am
☿ ℞ 1:51 pm
Color: Yellow

*Use a beech leaf in a healing amulet when
you've been hurt too often in love*

16 Thursday
1st ♋
Color: White

17 Friday
1st ♋
☽ v/c 6:27 am
☽ enters ♌ 12:52 pm
Color: Rose

Shavuot

Set in Eastern Standard Time (EST)

Hawthorn

Hawthorn is sacred to the old gods and goddesses of Ireland known as the Tuatha de Danaan. Long ago driven below the ground by foreign invaders, today the Tuatha de Danaan are the fairy folk of Ireland.

You can open yourself to fairy contact through a simple ritual. You will need two hawthorn blooms, a basket, and a chalice of water.

Go outside to a natural setting or garden and place the basket on the ground. Meditate on the setting's symbolism as a place of unity for two polarized forces; God-Goddess, male-female, fairy-human.

> *Fairies of old, I welcome your trust,*
> *I long to rekindle the bonds between us.*

Place the two hawthorn blooms in the basket, pour water over them, and walk away, leaving your offering of friendship to the fairies.

— Edain McCoy

---

18 Saturday
1st ♌
Color: Indigo

In recognition of the ancient Egyptians, burn the henna plant at sunset as incense to invoke the spirit of Ra

○ Sunday
1st ♌
2nd Quarter 2:42 pm
☽ v/c 3:34 pm
☽ enters ♍ 5:01 pm
Color: Gold

Pentecost

May

20 Monday
2nd ♍
♀ enters ♋ 8:27 am
Color: White

21 Tuesday
2nd ♍
☉ enters ♊ 12:29 am
☽ v/c 11:53 am
☽ enters ♎ 7:19 pm
Color: Red

Sun enters Gemini
Birthday of Gwyddion Pendderwen,
Pagan bard, 1946

22 Wednesday
2nd ♎
Color: Peach

Adoption of the Earth Religion
Anti-Abuse Act, 1988

23 Thursday
2nd ♎
☽ v/c 6:39 pm
☽ enters ♏ 8:38 pm
Color: Green

24 Friday
2nd ♏
Color: Pink

For general prosperity, coat a red candle
with honey and glitter; burn in tribute to
Fortuna, who teaches us about life and luck

Set in Eastern Standard Time (EST)

25 Saturday
2nd ♏
☽ v/c 8:20 pm
☽ enters ♐ 10:20 pm
Color: Gray

Scott Cunningham initiated into
the Traditional Gwyddonic
Order of the Wicca, 1981

Sunday
2nd ♐
Full Moon 6:51 am
Color: Orange

Flower Moon
Lunar Eclipse 7:04 am, 5° ♐ 04'

Set in Eastern Standard Time (EST)

May/June

27 Monday
3rd ♐
Color: Gray

Memorial Day (observed)
Birthday of Morning Glory
Zell, Church of All Worlds
Final confession of witchcraft by
Isobel Gowdie, Scotland, 1662

28 Tuesday
3rd ♐
☽ v/c 1:40 am
☽ enters ♑ 1:54 am
♂ enters ♋ 6:43 am
Color: Black

29 Wednesday
3rd ♑
☽ v/c 6:46 am
Color: Brown

Cloves, the plant of Juno, are excellent in spell crafting to banish debt

30 Thursday
3rd ♑
☽ enters ♒ 8:35 am
Color: Violet

Death of Joan of Arc, 1431

31 Friday
3rd ♒
Color: Peach

Flower Incense

Take equal parts of the following

Oak leaves
Nettle shoots
Burdock leaves
Broom flowers
Bean flowers
Horse chestnut blossoms
Meadowsweet flowers
Primrose flowers
Hawthorn blossoms
Blackthorn flowers
Corn cockle flowers

First crush oak leaves, nettle shoots, and burdock leaves together in a bowl or with a mortar and pestle. Then, add the flowers one by one and crush together until thoroughly blended.

— Anna Franklin

1 Saturday
3rd ♒
☽ v/c 4:19 pm
☽ enters ♓ 6:37 pm
Color: Gray

Witchcraft Act of 1563
takes effect in England

○ Sunday
3rd ♓
4th Quarter 7:05 pm
♅ ℞ 7:11 pm
Color: Yellow

Birthday of Alessandro
di Cagliostro, magician, 1743

Set in Eastern Standard Time (EST)

June

3 Monday
4th ♓
☽ v/c 5:58 am
Color: Lavender

To banish poverty, wash your clothes with angelica

4 Tuesday
4th ♓
☽ enters ♈ 6:51 am
Color: Gray

5 Wednesday
4th ♈
Color: Brown

6 Thursday
4th ♈
☽ v/c 4:47 pm
☽ enters ♉ 7:07 pm
Color: White

Prepare spells of fulfillment as the cycle of the wheel nears Summer Solstice—it is a particularly abundant time for love magic

7 Friday
4th ♉
Color: Rose

Green and Orange Salad

1 pound fresh or frozen green beans
1 cup grated carrot (about 2 carrots)
¼ cup roasted sunflower seeds
1 cup Oriental dressing
   (regular Italian works well, too)

Summer is the time for picnics, and this is one of my favorite dishes to make ahead of time and take to outdoor gatherings.

If you are using fresh green beans, prepare for cooking and steam about 10 minutes. If using frozen, prepare according to directions on the package. Drain thoroughly. While warm, mix with grated carrots and sunflower seeds, then add dressing and mix again. Refrigerate at least an hour.

— Magenta Griffith

---

8 Saturday
4th ♉
☿ D 10:12 am
Color: Indigo

---

9 Sunday
4th ♉
☽ v/c 3:14 am
☽ enters ♊ 5:29 am
Color: Gold

Birthday of Grace Cook, medium and founder of the White Eagle Lodge

Set in Eastern Standard Time (EST)

June

☽ Monday
4th ♊
New Moon 6:46 pm
Color: Silver

Solar Eclipse 6:48 pm, 19° ♊ 54'
Celtic Tree Month of Oak begins
Hanging of Bridget Bishop, first to
die in the Salem Witch trials, 1692

11 Tuesday
1st ♊
☽ v/c 11:05 am
☽ enters ♋ 1:15 pm
Color: Red

James I Witchcraft Statute replaces the
1563 mandate with stricter penalties, 1604

12 Wednesday
1st ♋
☿ enters ♍ 11:28 pm
Color: Peach

13 Thursday
1st ♋
☿ ℞ 12:50 pm
☽ v/c 4:44 pm
☽ enters ♌ 6:39 pm
Color: Turquoise

Birthday of Gerald Gardner, founder of
the Gardnerian Tradition
Birthday of William Butler Yeats, poet
and member of the Golden Dawn

14 Friday
1st ♌
♀ enters ♌ 3:16 pm
Color: Pink

Flag Day

Set in Eastern Standard Time (EST)

Oak

The mighty Oak Moon occurs at the time of the Summer Solstice, when the sun god is at his peak of strength and vitality. The Oak Moon offers us this same security, vigor, courage, and healing energy. The old Irish word for oak has often been translated as "door," giving us a glimpse into its power as a portal between all worlds.

To attain strength or healing during the Oak Moon, you will need two oak twigs and and two acorns. Hold a twig in each hand. Close your eyes and feel yourself being pulled to the center of all places as each twig leads you to a different world. When you feel you are at the oak's doorway, take an acorn in each hand; visualize one giving you strength, and the other taking away weakness or illness. Bury the acorn you feel is taking away your weakness—preferably at the base of an oak tree—and carry the other as a talisman of strength and well-being.

— Edain McCoy

15 Saturday
1st ♌
☽ v/c 8:17 pm
☽ enters ♍ 10:23 pm
Color: Blue

Margaret Jones becomes the first person executed as a Witch in the Massachusetts Bay Colony, 1648; she was a Boston doctor who was accused of witchcraft when several of her patients died

16 Sunday
1st ♍
Color: Orange

Father's Day

Set in Eastern Standard Time (EST)

June

☾ Monday
1st ♍
2nd Quarter 7:29 pm
☽ v/c 7:29 pm
Color: White

Birthday of Starhawk, Wiccan author

18 Tuesday
2nd ♍
☽ enters ♎ 1:11 am
Color: Black

Church of All Worlds
chartered with the IRS, 1970

19 Wednesday
2nd ♎
Color: Brown

Birthday of James I of England,
famous for his antiwitchcraft laws

Marriage of Margot Adler in the
first Wiccan handfasting to be carried in
the *New York Times* society pages, 1988

20 Thursday
2nd ♎
☽ v/c 1:38 am
☽ enters ♏ 3:42 am
Color: Violet

21 Friday
2nd ♏
☉ enters ♋ 8:24 am
Color: Peach

Midsummer/Litha/Summer Solstice
Sun enters Cancer

Set in Eastern Standard Time (EST)

Litha

Litha or the Summer Solstice sabbat celebrates the Sun at the peak of its power. The Sun and solstice are about male energy; and because fixed water power dominates on June 21, Mars triumphant will lend its energy to "increasing" projects and any magic begun at this time, such as money or prosperity spells. The Sun is waxing, the Moon is waxing, Mars is potent, and the day belongs to a smiling Venus! This is a wonderful holiday for lovers and their fertility.

Begin your ritual at dawn. Use sunflowers to represent the Sun King, but for Aphrodite decorate your altar with red roses, rose water, strawberries, and other aphrodisiacs. Burn dried clippings from your rose bushes for the cauldron fire. Spread rose butter on toast for cakes and ale, and sprinkle with fresh petals or rose scented sugar. To make rose butter, take a stick of butter and completely surround it in a small container with a cup of scented, organic, fresh red rose petals. Let the flavors marry overnight; discard petals and repeat.

— K. D. Spitzer

22 Saturday
2nd ♏
☽ v/c 4:27 am
☽ enters ♐ 6:42 am
Color: Gray

Final witchcraft law in England repealed, 1951

23 Sunday
2nd ♐
Color: Yellow

Integrate ginger into healing spell work; it is a wonder for soothing coughs and colds

Set in Eastern Standard Time (EST)

June

☺ Monday
2nd ♐
☽ v/c 8:38 am
☽ enters ♑ 11:01 am
Full Moon 4:42 pm
Color: White

Strong Sun Moon
Lunar Eclipse 4:28 pm, 3° ♑ 11'
Birthday of Janet Farrar, Wiccan author
James I Witchcraft Statute of 1604 is replaced in 1763 with a law against pretending to practice divination and witchcraft; law stands until 1951

25 Tuesday
3rd ♑
Color: Red

A law is introduced in Germany by Archbishop Siegfried III to encourage conversion rather than burning of heretics, 1233

26 Wednesday
3rd ♑
☽ v/c 2:37 am
☽ enters ♒ 5:36 pm
Color: Peach

Birthday of Stewart Farrar, Wiccan author
Richard of Gloucester assumes the English throne after accusing the widowed queen of Edward IV of witchcraft

27 Thursday
3rd ♒
Color: Green

Birthday of Scott Cunningham, Wiccan author

28 Friday
3rd ♒
Color: Pink

Set in Eastern Standard Time (EST)

29 Saturday
3rd ♒
☽ v/c 12:12 am
☽ enters ♓ 3:00 am
Color: Indigo

30 Sunday
3rd ♓
Color: Gold

To encourage your ideas to take flight, rub a mugwort-dragonsblood concoction on your third eye

Set in Eastern Standard Time (EST)

July

1 Monday
3rd ♓
☽ v/c 12:43 am
☽ enters ♈ 2:49 pm
Color: Gray

When seeking new beginnings, pay homage to the sylphs, guardians of the east; offer yellow cakes and lemonade and decorate your altar with yellow flowers and candles

2 Tuesday
3rd ♈
4th Quarter 12:19 pm
Color: White

3 Wednesday
4th ♈
Color: Yellow

Trial of Joan Prentice, who was accused of sending an imp in the form of a ferret to bite children; she allegedly had two imps named Jack and Jill, 1549

4 Thursday
4th ♈
☽ v/c 12:11 am
☽ enters ♉ 3:16 am
Color: Turquoise

Independence Day

5 Friday
4th ♉
Color: Pink

Conviction of Witches at third of four famous trials at Chelmsford, England, 1589

Set in Eastern Standard Time (EST)

Midsummer Incense

3 parts red sandalwood
1 part dried orange peel
1 part marigold petals

With mortar and pestle, crush sandalwood into a fine powder. Add dried orange peel and blend until thoroughly mixed. Finally, add ground marigold petals. Burn on a small charcoal block.

— Anna Franklin

6 Saturday
4th ♉
☽ v/c 10:57 am
☽ enters ♊ 2:01 pm
Color: Indigo

Scott Cunningham is initiated into
the Ancient Pictish Gaelic Way, 1981

7 Sunday
4th ♊
☿ enters ♋ 5:35 am
Color: Yellow

Set in Eastern Standard Time (EST)

July

8 Monday
4th ♊
☽ v/c 6:37 pm
☽ enters ♋ 9:36 pm
Color: White

Celtic Tree Month of Holly

9 Tuesday
4th ♋
Color: Red

Birthday of Amber K, Wiccan author
Death of Herman Slater,
proprietor of Magickal Childe
bookstore in New York, 1992

☽ Wednesday
4th ♋
New Moon 5:26 am
♀ enters ♍ 4:09 pm
☽ v/c 11:25 pm
Color: White

11 Thursday
1st ♋
☽ enters ♌ 2:08 am
Color: Green

12 Friday
1st ♌
Color: Rose

Plant a tree in the memory of a deceased friend or family member; this tribute is a powerful link between spirits and earth

Holly

The Celts saw holly as having a masculine energy, projective and fiery. It provided the user with a direct link to the energy of the gods.

Make sure your magical desire is clear in your mind, seen by only you and unseen by all others. With your goal clearly in mind, take twelve holly sprigs and separate them into bunches of three. Wrap three of these bunches in cloths of colors representing your goal. You may choose one color, or two, or three. As you wrap each bunch, say:

> *Holly red and holly white,*
> *Caring for my wish tonight;*
> *Holly strong and holly green,*
> *Bright to sight the now unseen.*

Garnish the bundles with the remaining holly sprigs and keep them covered and close to your sleeping place.

— Edain McCoy

---

13 Saturday
1st ♌
☽ v/c 1:42 am
☽ enters ♍ 4:41 am
♂ enters ♌ 10:23 am
Color: Brown

Birthday of Dr. John Dee, magician
Birthday of Dr. Margaret Murray, Egyptologist

---

14 Sunday
1st ♍
Color: Peach

First crop circles recorded on Silbury Hill, 1988

Set in Eastern Standard Time (EST)

July

15 Monday
1st ♍
☽ v/c 12:08 am
☽ enters ♎ 6:39 am
Color: Lavender

○ Tuesday
1st ♎
2nd Quarter 11:47 pm
Color: White

*Spice has natural antiseptic properties;
use ground cinnamon in a remedy
recipe for cuts and scrapes*

17 Wednesday
2nd ♎
☽ v/c 5:58 am
☽ enters ♏ 9:13 am
Color: Brown

First airing of *The Witching Hour*, a
Pagan radio show hosted by Winter
Wren and Don Lewis, on station
WONX in Evanston, Illinois, 1992

18 Thursday
2nd ♏
Color: Violet

19 Friday
2nd ♏
☽ v/c 9:35 am
☽ enters ♐ 1:02 pm
Color: White

Rebecca Nurse hanged in
Salem, Massachusetts, 1692

Set in Eastern Standard Time (EST)

20 Saturday
2nd ♐
Color: Blue

Pope Adrian VI issues a bull to the Inquisition to re-emphasize the 1503 bull of Julius II calling for the purging of "sorcerers by fire and sword," 1523

Lord Hunterford of England executed for treason for consulting Mother Roche, a Witch, and speculating on the king's death, 1540

21 Sunday
2nd ♐
☽ v/c 2:44 pm
☿ enters ♌ 5:41 pm
☽ enters ♑ 6:26 pm
Color: Orange

Set in Eastern Standard Time (EST)

July

22 Monday
2nd ♑
⚷ enters ♌ 10:26 am
☉ enters ♌ 7:15 pm
Color: Gray

Sun enters Leo
Northamptonshire Witches condemned, 1612
First modern recorded sighting of the Loch Ness Monster, 1930

23 Tuesday
2nd ♑
☽ v/c 10:05 pm
Color: Black

☺ Wednesday
2nd ♑
☽ enters ♒ 1:40 am
Full Moon 4:07 am
Color: Peach

Blessing Moon

25 Thursday
3rd ♒
Color: Turquoise

Death of Pope Innocent VIII, who issued bull *Summis Desiderantes Affectibus*, 1492

26 Friday
3rd ♒
☽ v/c 6:47 am
☽ enters ♓ 11:04 am
Color: Peach

Confession of Chelmsford Witches at first of four famous trials at Chelmsford, 1566; the others were held in 1579, 1589, and 1645; "Witch Finder General" Matthew Hopkins presided at the 1645 trials

Set in Eastern Standard Time (EST)

Lammas Incense

2 parts frankincense
2 parts benzoin
3 drops pine oil
1 part oak wood
½ part borage
½ part gorse flowers
½ part basil

In a bowl or with mortar and pestle, mix frankincense and benzoin, then add pine oil. Next blend oak wood and borage. Last, add crushed gorse flowers and basil. Burn on a charcoal block.

— Anna Franklin

27 Saturday
3rd ♓
Color: Indigo

Jennet Preston becomes the first of the "Malkin Tower" Witches to be hung; she was convicted of hiring Witches to help her murder Thomas Lister, 1612

28 Sunday
3rd ♓
☽ v/c 9:01 pm
☽ enters ♈ 10:39 pm
Color: Gold

Set in Eastern Standard Time (EST)

July/August

29 Monday
3rd ♈
Color: Silver

Agnes Waterhouse, one of the Chelmsford Witches, is hanged under the new witchcraft statute of Elizabeth I, 1566; she was accused of having a spotted cat familiar named Sathan

30 Tuesday
3rd ♈
Color: Red

Conrad of Marburg is murdered on the open road, presumably because he had shifted from persecuting poor heretics to nobles, 1233

31 Wednesday
3rd ♈
☽ v/c 10:48 am
☽ enters ♉ 11:17 am
Color: Brown

Date of fabled meeting of British Witches to raise cone of power to stop Hitler's invasion of England, 1940
Birthday of H. P. Blavatsky, founder of the Theosophical Society

○ Thursday
3rd ♉
4th Quarter 5:22 am
♃ enters ♌ 12:20 pm
Color: Green

Lammas/Lughnasadh
Birthday of Edward Kelly, medium of Dr. John Dee, 1555
AURORA Network UK founded, 2000

2 Friday
4th ♉
☽ v/c 5:58 pm
☽ enters ♊ 10:46 pm
Color: Peach

Birthday of Henry Steele Olcott, who cofounded the Theosophical Society with H. P. Blavatsky

Set in Eastern Standard Time (EST)

Lammas

Lammas is the first of the harvest festivals and this year, despite the fiery Sun, it has a strong, sensual feel of cardinal earth. Mars lends masculine energy to the Sun this week to help with the organizing for this bread festival. Round cornbread as a solar disk is an apt and easy choice for the altar, but if you plan several days ahead, you can sprout a small amount (¼ cup) of wheat or barley for kitchen witchery. Add this to other grains to your own bread made from scratch; or buy frozen bread dough, thaw, pat into a rectangle, and sprinkle with the sprouted grains. Roll up your dough like a jelly roll and place in a greased bread pan into which you have sprinkled Irish oats. You can use a sharp knife to carve goddess symbols into the loaf before baking.

— K. D. Spitzer

3 Saturday
4th ♊
Color: Blue

4 Sunday
4th ♊
Color: Gold

For tender dreams of sweet love
and a wedding to follow, fill your
home with honeysuckle

Set in Eastern Standard Time (EST)

August

5 Monday
4th ♊
☽ v/c 3:42 am
☽ enters ♋ 7:02 am
Color: White

Celtic Tree Month of Hazel begins

6 Tuesday
4th ♋
☿ enters ♍ 4:51 am
Color: Black

If you dream of a periwinkle, a spirit is looking out for your safety and well-being

7 Wednesday
4th ♋
♀ enters ♎ 4:09 am
☽ enters ♌ 11:27 am
Color: Peach

☽ Thursday
4th ♌
New Moon 2:15 pm
Color: Violet

Lammas cross-quarter day
(Sun reaches 15° Leo)

9 Friday
1st ♌
☽ v/c 8:36 am
☽ enters ♍ 1:03 pm
Color: Rose

Set in Eastern Standard Time (EST)

Hazel

The energy of the Hazel Moon is good for contacting spirits and for enhancing shapeshifting or astral projection rituals. It has a solid reputation of protective energy, especially useful for the protection of travelers. Hazel wood also makes an excellent shield for deflecting negative intent when made with this goal in mind.

To craft a simplified version of a hazel shield to protect yourself, your home or office, your car, or your barn, you will need at least nine hazel nuts, some thin cord in gold or white, and a hammer and nail. Empower the nuts as emblems of protection. Hammer a hole through them large enough for the cord, then string them together, making a binding knot between each. Hang these in your home and say,

> *Hazel, raise the shield so high,*
> *So tall and wide that none slips by;*
> *Protect, deflect, and quell all bane,*
> *Make all around me safe again.*

— Edain McCoy

10 Saturday
1st ♍
Color: Indigo

Open your heart in order to strive for your highest potential; drink from a chalice filled with red wine and envision yourself bathed in illuminating white light

11 Sunday
1st ♍
☽ v/c 7:01 am
☽ enters ♎ 1:38 pm
Color: Orange

Laurie Cabot withdraws from Salem, Massachusetts, mayoral race, 1987

Set in Eastern Standard Time (EST)

August

12 Monday
1st ♎
Color: Silver

*Use sweet pea oil in a gift
presented to a best friend*

13 Tuesday
1st ♎
☿ ℞ 9:59 am
☽ v/c 10:11 am
☽ enters ♏ 3:01 pm
Color: Gray

Aradia de Toscano allegedly
born in Volterra, Italy, 1313
Church of Wicca founded in Australia
by Lady Tamara Von Forslun, 1989

14 Wednesday
1st ♏
Color: Brown

☽ Thursday
1st ♏
2nd Quarter 5:12 am
☽ v/c 1:13 pm
☽ enters ♐ 6:25 pm
Color: Turquoise

Birthday of Charles Godfrey Leland,
author of *Aradia, Gospel of Witches*, 1824

16 Friday
2nd ♐
Color: Pink

Set in Eastern Standard Time (EST)

Savory Corn Bread

1 cup corn meal
1 cup flour
4 teaspoons baking powder
½ teaspoon salt
½ teaspoon sage
1 egg
1 cup milk
¼ cup vegetable oil
½ cup fresh, frozen, or canned corn

It's too hot to have the oven on for long this time of year, so this bakes quickly. It's best with fresh sweet corn, which is usually available by the first of August.

Grease a 8 x 8 pan and preheat oven to 425°. Mix dry ingredients and set aside. Mix wet ingredients in a separate container and add to dry ingredients all at once. Mix only until blended—it may be slightly lumpy. Stir in corn. Pour into pan, and bake for 20–25 minutes. This can be served warm or cold.

— Magenta Griffith

---

17 Saturday
2nd ♐
☽ v/c 6:39 pm
Color: Brown

Scott Cunningham's first initiation into Wicca, 1973

---

18 Sunday
2nd ♐
☽ enters ♑ 12:15 am
Color: Peach

Father Urbain Grandier found guilty of bewitching nuns at a convent in Loudoun, France, 1634

August

19 Monday
2nd ♑
☽ v/c 3:13 pm
Color: Gray

John Willard and Reverend George Burroughs put to death in the Salem Witch trials, 1692

20 Tuesday
2nd ♑
☽ enters ♒ 8:16 am
Color: Black

Execution of Lancashire Witches, 1612
Birthday of Ann Moura, Wiccan author
Birthday of H. P. Lovecraft, horror writer and alleged magician

21 Wednesday
2nd ♒
Color: White

☺ Thursday
2nd ♒
Full Moon 5:29 pm
☽ v/c 5:29 pm
☽ enters ♓ 6:11 pm
Color: Green

Corn Moon
Order of the Rosy Cross established, 1623
Pope John XXII, one of the first popes to promote the theory that witchcraft was heresy, orders the Inquisition at Carcassonne to seize the property of Witches, sorcerers, and those who make wax images, 1320

23 Friday
3rd ♓
☉ enters ♍ 2:17 am
Color: White

Sun enters Virgo

24 Saturday
3rd ♓
Color: Indigo

25 Sunday
3rd ♓
☽ v/c 1:58 am
☽ enters ♈ 5:48 am
Color: Yellow

Set in Eastern Standard Time (EST)

August/September

26 Monday
3rd ♈
♇ D 6:01 am
☿ enters ♎ 4:10 pm
Color: White

Cook with cumin: It helps to keep a
lover faithful and maintains
a peaceful environment at home

27 Tuesday
3rd ♈
☽ v/c 4:18 pm
☽ enters ♉ 6:32 pm
Color: Red

28 Wednesday
3rd ♉
Color: Brown

29 Thursday
3rd ♉
♂ enters ♍ 9:38 am
☽ v/c 11:44 pm
Color: White

Birthday of Pope Innocent VIII, who
issued bull Summis Desiderantes Affectibus

◑ Friday
3rd ♉
☽ enters ♊ 6:45 am
4th Quarter 9:31 pm
Color: Peach

If you sense danger while out and about,
cross a bridge or wade through a stream
as a protective shield: moving water
cancels negative intentions

Autumn Incense

3 parts myrrh
1 part blackthorn wood
1 part rowan berries
½ part galangal
½ part chervil
½ part vervain
½ part parsley

In a bowl or with a mortar and pestle, crush blackthorn wood into myrrh and stir until well blended. Add rowan berries, galangal, and chervil into the mixture. Last, add vervain and parsley, and grind mixture until thoroughly blended. Burn on a small charcoal block.

— Anna Franklin

31 Saturday
4th ♊
Color: Blue

Birthday of Raymond Buckland, who, along with his wife Rosemary, is generally credited with bringing Gardnerian Wicca to the United States

1 Sunday
4th ♊
☽ v/c 11:55 am
☽ enters ♋ 4:14 pm
Color: Yellow

September

2 Monday
4th ♋
Color: Lavender

Labor Day
Celtic Tree Month of Vine begins
Birthday of Reverend Paul
Beyerl, Wiccan author

3 Tuesday
4th ♋
☽ v/c 3:31 pm
☽ enters ♌ 9:36 pm
Color: Gray

*To be perceived as elegant,
wear the fragrance of jasmine*

4 Wednesday
4th ♌
Color: Peach

5 Thursday
4th ♌
☿ enters ♎ 2:15 pm
☽ v/c 8:33 pm
☽ enters ♍ 11:16 pm
Color: Violet

☽ Friday
4th ♍
New Moon 10:10 pm
Color: Peach

*Include the powerful essence
of dandelions in divination rituals*

Set in Eastern Standard Time (EST)

Vine

The Vine Moon coincides with the Autumnal Equinox, when the bounty of the harvest is celebrated. Fruits and wines are central to the holiday feast, and a portion is always sacrificed to the God and Goddess, whose union produced the harvest. The Vine Moon's energies are also used for seeking the blessing of inspiration from the deities.

You will need wine or fruit juice, an apple (symbolic of wisdom and sacred to the Crone Goddess who rules in autumn), a sharp knife, and a long pin or nail. Make a wine toast to the God and Goddess, offering it as a gift to them. Visualize the God and Goddess filling the wine with the essence of unity. Take the knife and slice the apple crosswise to reveal the five-pointed pentagram inside. Pour some of the wine into the center of the apple, and reseal the apple with the pin. Keep it through autumn as a talisman to draw to you both wisdom and divine inspiration.

— Edain McCoy

---

7 Saturday
1st ♍
⚷ D 8:21 am
☽ v/c 7:54 pm
♀ enters ♏ 10:05 pm
☽ enters ♎ 10:57 pm
Color: Brown

Rosh Hashanah

8 Sunday
1st ♎
Color: Gold

Founding of the Theosophical Society by H. P. Blavatsky, Henry Steele Olcott, and others, 1875

September

9 Monday
1st ♎
☽ v/c 7:52 pm
☽ enters ♏ 10:48 pm
Color: Gray

10 Tuesday
1st ♏
Color: Black

Birthday of Carl Llewellyn
Weschcke, owner and president
of Llewellyn Worldwide

11 Wednesday
1st ♏
☽ v/c 5:52 pm
Color: Brown

Birthday of Silver RavenWolf,
Wiccan author

Birthday of the Wiccan Pagan
Press Alliance (WPPA)

12 Thursday
1st ♏
☽ enters ♐ 12:44 am
Color: Green

☽ Friday
1st ♐
2nd Quarter 1:08 pm
Color: Pink

*If a rowan tree takes root in your yard, all
who dwell on the property will be blessed*

Set in Eastern Standard Time (EST)

14 Saturday
2nd ♐
☽ v/c 2:54 am
☽ enters ♑ 5:47 am
☿ ℞ 2:39 pm
Color: Blue

Phillip IV of France draws up the order for the arrest of the French Templars, 1306

Birthday of Henry Cornelius Agrippa, scholar and magician, 1486

15 Sunday
2nd ♑
Color: Peach

September

16 Monday
2nd ♑
☽ v/c 12:58 am
☽ enters ♒ 1:54 pm
Color: Silver

Yom Kippur

17 Tuesday
2nd ♒
Color: White

Bewitched debuts on ABC–TV, 1964

18 Wednesday
2nd ♒
☽ v/c 9:35 pm
Color: Yellow

19 Thursday
2nd ♒
☽ enters ♓ 12:18 am
Color: Turquoise

20 Friday
2nd ♓
Color: White

Honor the departed spirit of the
Corn King at the time of the Harvest
Moon with corn dollies and corn bread

Set in Eastern Standard Time (EST)

Mabon

At Mabon, the power of the Sun King is waning, and the harvest is in full swing. On September 23, the energies are fire and air, and the Moon is full. Allow for some mixups caused by retrograde Mercury when making your plans. Celebrate this Sabbat the night before, as the Harvest Moon begins to rise. Cover the altar with fall leaves and sumac berries. Bake nut bread as a symbol of the season.

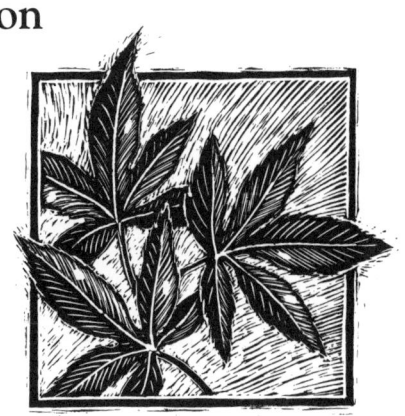

To make a fall chaplet, measure floral wire around your head and wrap the oval with brown floral tape. Using fall leaves and tape, carefully secure short stems or single leaves closely around the taped wire. Use leaves that you have dried or preserved. The hips of wild roses can add color. Tie a ribbon to drape down your back.

To preserve leaves, choose those at the height of autumn's color. Mix well one part glycerin with two parts very hot water. Make a vertical cut in woody stems and let them stand in the mixture. After a couple days, lay leaves flat in a container and pour the mixture over them. The leaves will shortly become pliable.

—K. D. Spitzer

Saturday
2nd ♓
Full Moon 8:59 am
☽ v/c 9:36 am
☽ enters ♈ 12:11 pm
Color: Indigo

Harvest Moon
Sukkot begins

22 Sunday
3rd ♈
☉ enters ♎ 11:55 pm
Color: Orange

Mabon/Fall Equinox
Sun enters Libra

Set in Eastern Standard Time (EST)

September

23 Monday
3rd ♈
☽ v/c 10:29 pm
Color: White

24 Tuesday
3rd ♈
☽ enters ♉ 12:55 am
Color: Red

25 Wednesday
3rd ♉
Color: Brown

Senate passes an amendment (705) attached by Senator Jesse Helms to House Resolution 3036 (1986 budget bill), denying tax exempt status to any organization that espouses satanism or witchcraft, 1985

26 Thursday
3rd ♉
☽ v/c 4:27 am
☽ enters ♊ 1:26 pm
Color: Green

Joan Wiliford hanged at Faversham, England, 1645; she testified that the Devil came to her in the form of a black dog that she called "Bunnie"

27 Friday
3rd ♊
☿ enters ♍ 8:20 am
Color: Rose

Sukkot ends

Set in Eastern Standard Time (EST)

Mabon Incense

2 parts benzoin
2 parts myrrh
1 part hazelwood
½ part corn
½ part cornflower
½ part ivy
½ part red poppy flowers

In a bowl or with mortar and pestle blend benzoin and myrrh with hazelwood. Next add cornflower, and stir until thoroughly mixed. Crush dried corn and ivy into the mixture, and add poppy flowers. Burn on a small charcoal block.

— Anna Franklin

28 Saturday
3rd ♊
☽ v/c 10:01 pm
Color: Gray

○ Sunday
3rd ♊
☽ enters ♋ 12:01 am
4th Quarter 12:03 pm
Color: Yellow

Wear a garland of ivy in your locks to prevent hair loss following an illness

September/October

30 Monday
4th ♋
☽ v/c 1:59 pm
Color: Lavender

Celtic Tree Month of Ivy begins

1 Tuesday
4th ♋
☽ enters ♌ 6:58 am
Color: Gray

Birthday of Isaac Bonewitz,
Druid, magician, and Witch

Birthday of Annie Besant,
Theosophical Society president

2 Wednesday
4th ♌
☿ enters ♍ 4:26 am
Color: Brown

Birthday of Timothy Roderick,
Wiccan author

3 Thursday
4th ♌
☽ v/c 8:16 am
☽ enters ♍ 9:52 am
Color: Violet

4 Friday
4th ♍
Color: Peach

President Reagan signs JR 165 making 1983 "The Year of the Bible" (public law #9728Q); the law states that the Bible is the word of God and urges a return to "traditional" Christian values, 1982

Set in Eastern Standard Time (EST)

Ivy

Ivy is as feminine as holly is masculine—their roles as emblems of the universal creator are preserved for us in the medieval Christmas hymn, "The Holly and the Ivy." The Ivy Moon strengthens our inner resilience.

Begin your ritual of exorcism inside a protective circle into which you have invited all the elemental spirits and the wise crone Goddess. On a small piece of paper, write down that which you wish to banish. Lightly dab patchouli oil around the edge to help ground its negative influence. Dab rosemary oil on your breastbone to help you bounce back from this challenge.

Burn the paper in a heat-resistant bowl and say:

> *Banished be (insert name of problem), the blight;*
> *Burned to ash and buried this night.*

Bury the ashes from the bowl outside under a strong tree, and cover the spot with ivy leaves.

— Edain McCoy

---

5 Saturday
4th ♍
☽ v/c 8:22 am
☽ enters ♎ 9:51 am
Color: Brown

Sunday
4th ♎
New Moon 6:18 am
☿ D 2:28 pm
Color: Gold

October

7 Monday
1st ♎
☽ v/c 7:29 am
☽ enters ♏ 8:57 am
Color: White

Birthday of Arnold Crowther, stage magician and Gardnerian Witch, 1909

8 Tuesday
1st ♏
Color: Black

Create a magical vessel/pouch that you can turn to whenever you are in need of comfort, sustenance, and vision; fill with aromatic herbs that you find pleasing to your senses

9 Wednesday
1st ♏
☿ D 12:56 am
☽ v/c 7:38 am
☽ enters ♐ 9:21 am
Color: Peach

10 Thursday
1st ♐
♀ ℞ 1:35 pm
Color: Green

11 Friday
1st ♐
☿ enters ♎ 12:56 am
♄ ℞ 8:01 am
☽ v/c 11:08 am
☽ enters ♑ 12:45 pm
Color: Pink

Apple Crisp

4 large apples, peeled, cored, and sliced
⅓ cup flour or oat flour
1 cup rolled oats
½ cup brown sugar
2 teaspoons cinnamon
¼ teaspoon nutmeg
¼ cup (half a stick) butter

I love to go apple-picking in the fall. I always get more apples than I can eat, so I have plenty for dishes like this.

Preheat oven to 375°. Put apples in a buttered pie plate or baking dish. Mix dry ingredients. Cut butter into mixture with a pastry blender. Spread the mixture evenly over apples and bake for 30 minutes or until top is golden brown. Serve warm, with ice cream.

— Magenta Griffith

12 Saturday
1st ♑
Color: Gray

Birthday of Aleister Crowley

☽ Sunday
1st ♑
2nd Quarter 12:33 am
☽ v/c 5:42 pm
☽ enters ♒ 7:51 pm
Color: Orange

Jacques de Molay and other French Templars arrested by order of King Phillip IV, 1306

Set in Eastern Standard Time (EST)

October

14 Monday
2nd ♒
Color: Silver

Columbus Day (observed)

15 Tuesday
2nd ♒
♂ enters ♎ 12:38 pm
Color: White

To avert sorrow when a single magpie flies westward, Gypsy lore suggests you acknowledge its presence by saying, "Good day, Your Lordship"; for further protection against the winged messenger, leave an offering of food and a shiny object

16 Wednesday
2nd ♒
☽ v/c 4:15 am
☽ enters ♓ 6:07 am
Color: Yellow

17 Thursday
2nd ♓
Color: Turquoise

18 Friday
2nd ♓
☽ v/c 4:17 pm
☽ enters ♈ 6:13 pm
Color: White

Birthday of Nicholas Culpepper, astrologer and herbalist

Set in Eastern Standard Time (EST)

19 Saturday
2nd ♈
Color: Indigo

To instill a sense of playfulness, create a fragrance that incorporates ylang-ylang, which is known to energize hope and dismiss anxiety

20 Sunday
2nd ♈
♆ D 8:53 am
Color: Peach

Birthday of Selena Fox, Circle Sanctuary

October

☺ Monday
2nd ♈
Full Moon 2:20 am
☽ v/c 4:55 am
☽ enters ♉ 6:57 am
Color: Gray

Blood Moon

22 Tuesday
3rd ♉
Color: Black

23 Wednesday
3rd ♉
☽ v/c 9:14 pm
☉ enters ♏ 9:18 am
☽ enters ♊ 7:17 pm
Color: Brown

Sun enters Scorpio

24 Thursday
3rd ♊
Color: White

25 Friday
3rd ♊
Color: Pink

Jacques de Molay first interrogated
after Templar arrest, 1306

Set in Eastern Standard Time (EST)

Reed

The Reed Moon is connected to the solar festival of Samhain, the time when we are open to contact with ancestor spirits, strengthen our family ties, and gather in supplies for the winter ahead.

First, take time to collect items you feel link you to your ancestors and place these objects on an altar. Light a candle for each spirit whose name you call aloud, then light one more for friendly wandering spirits. Once you sense their presence, offer them food and drink.

Thank the spirits for making sacrifices that made your world a better place, and for giving you stamina to cope with adversity. Think of all the positive aspects of yourself and honor them with blessings. For example:

> *Blessed be they who made me tall and redheaded.*
> *Blessed be they who made me smart and patient.*
> *Blessed be they who gave me artistic talent.*
> *Blessed be they who gave me a sense of humor. . . .*

— Edain McCoy

---

26 Saturday
3rd ♊
☽ v/c 4:01 am
☽ enters ♋ 6:10 am
Color: Blue

Sibyl Leek dies of cancer, 1982
De Molay and thirty-one other Templars confess to heresy in front of an assembly of clergy; all later recant their confessions, 1306

---

27 Sunday
3rd ♋
Color: Yellow

Daylight Saving Time ends at 2 am
Circle Sanctuary founded, 1974

October/November

28 Monday
3rd ♋
☽ v/c 3:22 am
☽ enters ♌ 2:20 pm
Color: Lavender

Celtic Tree Month of Reed begins

○ Tuesday
3rd ♌
4th Quarter 12:28 am
Color: Red

MacGregor Mathers issues manifesto calling himself supreme leader of the Golden Dawn; all members had to sign an oath of fealty to him, 1896

Birthday of Frater Zarathustra, who founded the Temple of Truth in 1972

30 Wednesday
4th ♌
☽ v/c 4:51 pm
☽ enters ♍ 6:59 pm
Color: Peach

House-Senate conferees drop the Senate provision barring the IRS from granting tax-exempt status to groups that promote satanism or witchcraft, stating that the provision came under the jurisdiction of the House Ways and Means Committee, 1985

31 Thursday
4th ♍
☿ enters ♏ 5:43 pm
Color: Green

Samhain/Halloween
Charter date for Covenant of the Goddess
New Reformed Orthodox Order of the Golden Dawn formed, 1967
Martin Luther nails his ninety-five theses to the door of Wittenburg Castle Church, igniting the Protestant revolution, 1517

1 Friday
4th ♍
☽ v/c 6:19 pm
☽ enters ♎ 8:28 pm
Color: Peach

All Saints' Day
Aquarian Tabernacle Church established in the United States, 1979

Set in Eastern Standard Time (EST)

Samhain/Halloween

Samhain grows in strength as a holiday, and while its meanings may be obscure to the general public, many rituals have survived intact. This is Hecate's day, a celebration of the crone and the powers of the dark feminine principle. This is the day of the dead; you can honor your ancestors by setting a place for them at the table. Add their pictures to your altar. Indulge in wearing and decorating with black. Bring all your mojo to the altar to recharge.

With the veil between the worlds at its thinnest, a ritual at midnight on October 31 brings a last-quarter Moon and a very lucky Sun. Keep divination tools in your circle, and cast a spread to reveal the portents of the coming new year. Enhance your powers with a loose incense to burn on charcoal. Just blend a teaspoon each of crushed cinnamon, dittany of Crete, rosemary, and bay. Mix equal amounts dragon's blood and frankincense and add 1 part resin to 1 part mixed herbs.

— K. D. Spitzer

2 Saturday
4th ♎
Color: Blue

Circle Sanctuary purchases land for nature preserve, 1983

3 Sunday
4th ♎
☽ v/c 5:56 pm
☽ enters ♏ 8:10 pm
Color: Yellow

November

☽ Monday
4th ♏
♅ D 1:27 am
New Moon 3:34 pm
Color: Gray

When conducting fertility magic, sanctify
a pomegranate in the name of Juno

5 Tuesday
1st ♏
☽ v/c 11:48 am
☽ enters ♐ 8:01 pm
Color: Red

Election Day (general)

6 Wednesday
1st ♐
Color: Brown

Ramadan begins

7 Thursday
1st ♐
☽ v/c 7:14 pm
☽ enters ♑ 9:59 pm
Color: Green

8 Friday
1st ♑
Color: White

Samhain cross-quarter day
(Sun reaches 15° Scorpio)
Marriage of Patricia and Arnold Crowther
officiated by Gerald Gardner, 1960
Sentencing of Witches in Basque
Zugarramurdi trial, 1610

Set in Eastern Standard Time (EST)

Wild Rice Almondine

1 cup uncooked wild rice
4 tablespoons butter
1 onion, minced
2–4 cloves garlic, minced
½ pound mushrooms, chopped
½ cup almonds, chopped
3 cups broth (vegetarian or chicken)
Salt and pepper to taste

Soak the wild rice in boiling water for 1 hour. In a large frying pan, melt butter. Add the onions and garlic and sauté for 5 minutes. Add mushrooms, sauté 5 minutes more. Add nuts and cook another 5 minutes. Drain the rice and add to mushroom mixture. Add broth, and season. Pour entire mixture into a buttered 1½-quart casserole dish and bake covered for 1¼ hours. Uncover and bake 15 more minutes, or until liquid is completely absorbed. Serves 5–7.

— Magenta Griffith

9 Saturday
1st ♑
☽ v/c 3:22 am
Color: Brown

Patricia and Arnold Crowther
married in civil ceremony, 1960

10 Sunday
1st ♑
☽ enters ♒ 3:27 am
Color: Orange

November

☾ Monday
1st ♒
2nd Quarter 3:52 pm
Color: Silver

Veterans Day

12 Tuesday
2nd ♒
☽ v/c 9:06 am
☽ enters ♓ 12:42 pm
Color: Black

An old European custom is to remove a branch from a cherry tree at the onset of winter; kept in water near a hearth, the branch usually will bloom by the solstice

13 Wednesday
2nd ♓
Color: White

14 Thursday
2nd ♓
☽ v/c 8:38 pm
Color: Turquoise

15 Friday
2nd ♓
☽ enters ♈ 12:38 am
Color: Rose

Aquarian Tabernacle Church established in Canada, 1993

Death of Albertus Magnus, a ceremonial magician who allegedly discovered the philosopher's stone

16 Saturday
2nd ♈
Color: Gray

17 Sunday
2nd ♈
☽ v/c 9:06 am
☽ enters ♉ 1:23 pm
Color: Gold

Birthday of Israel Regardie, occultist
and member of the OTO, 1907

Set in Eastern Standard Time (EST)

November

18 Monday
2nd ♉
Color: White

Aleister Crowley initiated into the
Golden Dawn as Frater Perdurabo, 1898

☺ Tuesday
2nd ♉
☿ enters ♐ 6:29 am
Full Moon 8:34 pm
☽ v/c 8:34 pm
Color: Gray

Mourning Moon
Lunar Eclipse 8:46 pm, 27° ♉ 33'
Birthday of Theodore
Parker Mills, Wiccan elder

20 Wednesday
3rd ♉
☽ enters ♊ 1:25 am
Color: Peach

Church of All Worlds
incorporates in Australia, 1992

21 Thursday
3rd ♊
♀ D 2:12 am
Color: Green

22 Friday
3rd ♊
☉ enters ♐ 6:54 am
☽ v/c 7:07 am
☽ enters ♋ 11:48 am
Color: White

Sun enters Sagittarius
Phillip IV pressures Pope Clement to issue
bull *Pastoralis Praeminentiae* calling for
monarchs of Western Europe to arrest
any Templars in their territories, 1306;
Clement agrees after a high-level Templar
confesses he denied Christ at his reception

Set in Eastern Standard Time (EST)

Herne Incense

3 parts frankincense
3 drops oak moss oil
½ part pine resin
1 part oak bark
2 parts crushed juniper berries
½ part yarrow

In a bowl or with a mortar and pestle, blend frankincense, oil, and pine resin. Add oak bark, juniper berries, and yarrow, and crush together until well mixed. Burn on a charcoal block.

— Anna Franklin

23 Saturday
3rd ♋
Color: Indigo

Birthday of Lady Tamara Von Forslun, founder of the Church of Wicca and the Aquarian Tabernacle Church in Australia

24 Sunday
3rd ♋
☽ v/c 11:51 am
☽ enters ♌ 8:00 pm
Color: Peach

Set in Eastern Standard Time (EST)

November/December

25 Monday
3rd ♌
Color: Lavender

Celtic Tree Month of Elder begins
Dr. John Dee notes Edward
Kelly's death in his diary, 1595

26 Tuesday
3rd ♌
☽ v/c 8:51 pm
Color: Red

○ Wednesday
3rd ♌
☽ enters ♍ 1:42 am
4th Quarter 10:46 am
☿ enters ♏ 3:09 pm
Color: Yellow

Sacred to Bacchus, god of wine and revelry, ivy symbolized immortality to pagans; include ivy in rituals prior to celebratory gatherings

28 Thursday
4th ♍
Color: Violet

Thanksgiving Day

29 Friday
4th ♍
☽ v/c 12:01 am
☽ enters ♎ 4:54 am
Color: Peach

Set in Eastern Standard Time (EST)

Elder

The Elder Moon is both the end of the Celtic lunar year and a time to prepare for the next. The day after the Elder Moon resides in no month, but is a solemn spiritual day known as the Secret of the Unhewn Stone or the Feast of Potential.

During this Moon, plan to meet with your shadow self or cowalker—the part of you residing in the otherworld who is the key to your completeness. It reflects the true self of the year gone by, so that you may prepare to fulfill the potential of the year to come.

Turn your altar to the west and light one black and one white candle. Gaze between them into a portal to the otherworld. Call out to your other self to appear to you between the candles. When the image is visible, commune with it in whatever method seems appropriate. Learn from this self all you can about your true earthly nature.

Offer your shadow self food and drink before bidding it farewell.

— Edain McCoy

30 Saturday
4th ♎
Color: Gray

Hanukkah begins
Birthday of Oberon Zell,
Church of All Worlds
Father Urbain Grandier imprisoned in
France for bewitching nuns, 1633

1 Sunday
4th ♎
☽ v/c 6:06 am
☽ enters ♏ 6:15 am
♂ enters ♏ 9:26 am
Color: Gold

Birthday of Anodea Judith,
president, Church of All Worlds

Set in Eastern Standard Time (EST)

December

2 Monday
4th ♏
☽ v/c 11:15 pm
Color: Gray

Burn frankincense incense when consecrating ritual tools and objects

3 Tuesday
4th ♏
☽ enters ♐ 6:58 am
Color: Red

☿ Wednesday
4th ♐
New Moon 2:34 am
♃ ℞ 7:22 am
Color: Brown

Solar Eclipse 2:38 am, 11° ♐ 58'

5 Thursday
1st ♐
☽ v/c 2:55 am
☽ enters ♑ 8:39 am
☽ v/c 3:20 pm
Color: Green

Death of Aleister Crowley, 1947
Pope Innocent VIII reverses the *Canon Episcopi* by issuing the bull *Summis Desiderantes Affectibus*, removing obstacles to inquisitors, 1484

6 Friday
1st ♑
Color: Pink

Birthday of Dion Fortune, member of the Golden Dawn, 1890
Death of Jacob Sprenger, coauthor of the *Malleus Maleficarum*, 1495

Set in Eastern Standard Time (EST)

Orange Chocolate Chip Cookies

1¼ cups flour
½ teaspoon baking soda
¼ teaspoon salt
½ cup (1 stick) butter or margarine
½ cup white sugar
¼ cup brown sugar
1 egg
½ teaspoon vanilla
1 tablespoon finely grated orange peel
1 tablespoon frozen orange juice concentrate
1 cup chocolate chips

Combine flour, soda, and salt, and set aside. Cream the butter or margarine, add the sugars, and mix well. Add egg, vanilla, orange peel, and juice. Blend thoroughly. Add flour mixture, and beat until no flour is showing. Add the chocolate chips and mix. Drop by teaspoons on a greased baking sheet. Bake at 375° for 10 to 15 minutes.

— Magenta Griffith

7 Saturday
1st ♑
☽ enters ♒ 12:54 pm
Color: Brown

Hanukkah ends

8 Sunday
1st ♒
☿ enters ♑ 3:21 pm
Color: Yellow

Ramadan ends

Set in Eastern Standard Time (EST)

December

9 Monday
1st ≈
☽ v/c 1:35 pm
☽ enters ♓ 8:46 pm
Color: Lavender

*Foes who met under mistletoe in the forest would
sheathe their weaponry and maintain a truce for a day;
you can use the sacred herb in truce-making spells*

10 Tuesday
1st ♓
⚷ enters ♎ 9:52 am
Color: Black

☽ Wednesday
1st ♓
2nd Quarter 10:49 am
Color: White

12 Thursday
2nd ♓
☽ v/c 12:02 am
☽ enters ♈ 7:58 am
Color: Violet

13 Friday
2nd ♈
Color: Peach

First papal bull against black magic
issued by Alexander IV, 1258

Set in Eastern Standard Time (EST)

14 Saturday

2nd ♈
☽ v/c 12:18 pm
☽ enters ♉ 8:43 pm
Color: Gray

*Drink sassafras-infused tea for
good health and well-being*

15 Sunday

2nd ♉
Color: Orange

Set in Eastern Standard Time (EST)

December

16 Monday
2nd ♉
Color: White

17 Tuesday
2nd ♉
☽ v/c 12:11 am
☽ enters ♊ 8:43 am
Color: Gray

Use rosemary to ward against evil by strewing it on the floor at yuletide, as was the custom during the Middle Ages

18 Wednesday
2nd ♊
Color: Yellow

☺ Thursday
2nd ♊
Full Moon 2:10 pm
☽ v/c 2:10 pm
☽ enters ♋ 6:30 pm
Color: Turquoise

Long Nights Moon

20 Friday
3rd ♋
Color: White

The British Druids believed mistletoe could heal the sick, render poison harmless, dispel evil spirits, aid in conception, protect against storms, and bring good fortune

Set in Eastern Standard Time (EST)

Yule

Yule brings the longest night of the year and the rebirth of the Sun King. The energies of this Sabbat are very strong and very fertile in water and earth on December 21. Mars and Venus are united in Scorpio, and the Moon waxes full in her own sign, but then moves void-of-course. Celebrate the night before on Venus's day and enjoy all the pleasures of the flesh. Use a table-top balsam as your altar, and festoon it with all the glittery symbols of the elements and Lord and Lady. Anoint bayberry candles and burn them for prosperity and growth in the coming year. Make a sumptuous feast of comforting and magical foods. Smudge your altar with dried arbor vitae to waft your desires to the Goddess. Indulge your senses with the sights and smells of the season. Carve Sun symbols on last year's Yule log and burn it with chanting (bring back the light!).

Invite friends and family to the feasting to reveal the universality of your craft and the playful side of your spirituality. Reclaim the ancient pagan customs of the season.

— K. D. Spitzer

21 Saturday
3rd ♋
☽ v/c 4:31 am
☉ enters ♑ 8:14 pm
Color: Indigo

Yule/Winter Solstice
Sun enters Capricorn

22 Sunday
3rd ♋
☽ enters ♌ 1:48 am
Color: Peach

Janet and Stewart Farrar begin their first coven together, 1970

Set in Eastern Standard Time (EST)

December

23 Monday
3rd ♌
☽ v/c 11:58 pm
Color: Silver

In deference to the Druids, weave sprigs of holly into your hair just after Winter Solstice for the ceremonial cutting of the mistletoe

24 Tuesday
3rd ♌
☽ enters ♍ 7:05 am
Color: Red

Christmas Eve
Celtic Tree Month of Birch begins

25 Wednesday
3rd ♍
Color: Brown

Christmas Day
Feast of Frau Holle, Germanic weather goddess who was believed to travel through the world to watch people's deeds; she blessed the good and punished the bad

◐ Thursday
3rd ♍
☽ v/c 2:10 am
☽ enters ♎ 10:53 am
4th Quarter 7:31 pm
Color: Green

Kwanzaa begins
Dr. Fian arraigned for twenty counts of witchcraft and treason

27 Friday
4th ♎
Color: Rose

Birthday of Gerina Dunwich, Wiccan Author

Set in Eastern Standard Time (EST)

Birch

The Birch Moon prepares us for the journey through the year ahead. Purification and protection rituals are common practices as the year again begins its waxing phase.

Prepare yourself for things to come by making a birch broom. For the shaft choose any branch or dowel two to four feet in length. Attach birch twigs to one end using twine. Light thirteen candles, one for each of the thirteen Celtic Tree Months.

Rhythmically tap the broom over your body to purify your spirit and to garner a protective force around you. Think of losing the uneasy and unsettled elements of the past year while gaining those needed to make this year better. Do this to a chant.

> *Broom and birch my spirit free,*
> *Preparing me for what may be;*
> *The past is done, the future unformed,*
> *With purity and protection my path is adorned.*

— Edain McCoy

28 Saturday
4th ♎
☽ v/c 7:15 am
☽ enters ♏ 1:41 pm
Color: Blue

29 Sunday
4th ♏
Color: Gold

Set in Eastern Standard Time (EST)

December/January

30 Monday
4th ♏
☽ v/c 12:04 pm
☽ enters ♐ 4:01 pm
Color: Gray

31 Tuesday
4th ♐
Color: Black

New Year's Eve
Castle of Countess Bathory of Hungary raided, 1610; accused of practicing black magic, she murdered scores of the local townsfolk; she was walled up in a room in her castle, where she later died

1 Wednesday
4th ♐
☽ v/c 12:23 pm
☽ enters ♑ 6:42 pm
Color: Brown

New Year's Day
Kwanzaa ends

☽ Thursday
4th ♑
☿ ℞ 1:21 pm
New Moon 3:23 pm
Color: Green

3 Friday
1st ♑
☽ v/c 7:56 pm
☽ enters ♒ 10:56 pm
Color: White

Yuletide Incense

3 parts frankincense
3 drops orange oil
3 drops juniper oil
1 part crushed juniper berries
½ part mistletoe leaves

In a small bowl or with mortar and pestle blend frankincense with orange and juniper oils. Add crushed juniper berries and mistletoe, and mix until blended. Burn on a charcoal block. Mistletoe berries are poisonous when ingested, so exercise caution with any extra plant material.

— Anna Franklin

4 Saturday
1st ≈
Color: Gray

5 Sunday
1st ≈
Color: Yellow

About the Authors

THEA BLOOM is a professional intuitive who divides her time between Chicago and Los Angeles. As a workshop leader for Power Places Tours she gives seminars at sacred sites around the world, teaching individuals to use archetypal symbol systems, like the tarot, for self-transformation.

ESTELLE DANIELS is a Pagan minister and member of the Wiccan Church of Minnesota. She is also a professional part-time astrologer and author of *Astrologickal Magick*, and coauthor with Rev. Paul Tuitéan of *Pocket Guide to Wicca* and *Essential Wicca*. She has been practicing astrology professionally since 1972. She has been active in the Pagan community since 1989, travels to festivals, gives lectures, and works individually with students.

MARGUERITE ELSBETH, also known as Senihele (Sparrowhawk), is a hereditary Sicilian strega, and is also proud of her Lenni Lenape (Delaware) Indian ancestry. She is a professional astrologer, tarot reader, and spiritual healer. Marguerite is the author of *Crystal Medicine*, and coauthor of *The Grail Castle: Male Myths and Mysteries in the Celtic Tradition* and *The Silver Wheel: Women's Myths and Mysteries in the Celtic Tradition*.

ANNA FRANKLIN is the author of *The Sacred Circle Tarot*. She has also been a priestess of the British Pagan tradition since the age of eighteen. In 1986, Anna founded the Hearth of Arianrhod, which runs training and teaching circles and publishes a Pagan magazine called *Silver Wheel*. Anna now lives in a village in the English midlands and spends much of her time writing Pagan books, including *Herbcraft* (with Sue Lavender), *Pagan Feasts* (with Sue Phillips), *Fairy Lore*, and *Ritual Incenses and Oils*.

YASMINE GALENORN has practiced the Craft since 1980. She teaches classes on natural magic, leads public and private rituals, and is a professional tarot reader with a loyal clientele. She is the author of *Embracing the Moon, Trancing the Witch's Wheel,* and *Dancing with the Sun.*

MAGENTA GRIFFITH has been a Witch for over twenty-five years, a high priestess for over twelve years, and is a founding member of the coven Prodea, which has been practicing for nearly twenty years. She presents workshops and classes at festivals and gatherings around the Midwest.

LADY GYNGERE OF THE GROVE wrote the herbal sayings scattered throughout the datebook. A journalist and cookbook editor, Lady Gyngere is an internationally recognized authority on specialty food and beverages. She is the culinary delights columnist for *Renaissance Magazine*. Her expertise includes medieval kitchens and equipment, great hall feasting, courtly love, ale as a cultural artifact, and dining etiquette.

EDAIN MCCOY has been a Witch since 1981, and today is a part of the Wittan Irish Pagan tradition and a priestess of Brighid and elder within that tradition. Edain is the author of *Witta: An Irish Pagan Tradition; A Witch's Guide to Faery Folk; The Sabbats; Mountain Magic; Entering the Summerland; Inside A Witches' Coven;* and *Celtic Women's Spirituality.*

DOROTHY MORRISON is a third degree high priestess of the Georgian tradition, and has spent many years teaching the Craft to students across the United States and in Australia. She is the author of *Everyday Magic; In Praise of the Crone; Bud, Blossom & Leaf: A Magical Herb Gardener's Handbook; The Whimsical Tarot; The Craft;* and *The Craft Companion.*

JAMI SHOEMAKER has been practicing Witchcraft for eighteen years, and was initiated as a priestess in the Rowan Tree Church in 1992. She has taught a variety of Craft-related subjects, and has worked to help educate the general public about her religion. She has a degree in vocal music, a background in theater and dance, and has always enjoyed writing.

K. D. SPITZER has been a solitary practitioner for more than twenty years. Able to see fairies and other elementals as a child, she has developed this mystical side as an adult. She is an experienced astrologer, teacher, and writer, who uses astrological magic in her spell working.

WREN WALKER is the co-founder and chairperson of the Witches' Voice, Inc. Speaking as a lifelong Witch and civil rights activist, she has been interviewed on numerous radio programs, television shows, and many major newspapers. Wren facilitates workshops on Pagan rights issues at festivals throughout the country and also provides private spiritual counseling for Pagans who have been diagnosed with a terminal illness. She shares a home with TWV cofounder and husband Fritz Jung, and their two cats.

Name:

Address, City, State, Zip:

Home Phone: Office Phone:

E-mail: Birthday:

Name:

Address, City, State, Zip:

Home Phone: Office Phone:

E-mail: Birthday:

Name:

Address, City, State, Zip:

Home Phone: Office Phone:

E-mail: Birthday:

Name:

Address, City, State, Zip:

Home Phone: Office Phone:

E-mail: Birthday:

Name:

Address, City, State, Zip:

Home Phone: Office Phone:

E-mail: Birthday:

Name:

Address, City, State, Zip:

Home Phone: Office Phone:

E-mail: Birthday:

Name:

Address, City, State, Zip:

Home Phone: Office Phone:

E-mail: Birthday:

Name:

Address, City, State, Zip:

Home Phone: Office Phone:

E-mail: Birthday:

Name:

Address, City, State, Zip:

Home Phone: Office Phone:

E-mail: Birthday:

Name:

Address, City, State, Zip:

Home Phone: Office Phone:

E-mail: Birthday:

Name:

Address, City, State, Zip:

Home Phone: Office Phone:

E-mail: Birthday:

Name:

Address, City, State, Zip:

Home Phone: Office Phone:

E-mail: Birthday:

Name:

Address, City, State, Zip:

Home Phone: Office Phone:

E-mail: Birthday:

Name:

Address, City, State, Zip:

Home Phone: Office Phone:

E-mail: Birthday:

Name:

Address, City, State, Zip:

Home Phone: Office Phone:

E-mail: Birthday:

Name:

Address, City, State, Zip:

Home Phone: Office Phone:

E-mail: Birthday:

Name:

Address, City, State, Zip:

Home Phone: Office Phone:

E-mail: Birthday:

Name:

Address, City, State, Zip:

Home Phone: Office Phone:

E-mail: Birthday:

Name:

Address, City, State, Zip:

Home Phone: Office Phone:

E-mail: Birthday:

Name:

Address, City, State, Zip:

Home Phone: Office Phone:

E-mail: Birthday:

Name:

Address, City, State, Zip:

Home Phone: Office Phone:

E-mail: Birthday:

Name:

Address, City, State, Zip:

Home Phone: Office Phone:

E-mail: Birthday:

Name:

Address, City, State, Zip:

Home Phone: Office Phone:

E-mail: Birthday:

Name:

Address, City, State, Zip:

Home Phone: Office Phone:

E-mail: Birthday:

Name:

Address, City, State, Zip:

Home Phone: Office Phone:

E-mail: Birthday:

Name:

Address, City, State, Zip:

Home Phone: Office Phone:

E-mail: Birthday:

Name:

Address, City, State, Zip:

Home Phone: Office Phone:

E-mail: Birthday:

Name:

Address, City, State, Zip:

Home Phone: Office Phone:

E-mail: Birthday:

Name:

Address, City, State, Zip:

Home Phone: Office Phone:

E-mail: Birthday:

Name:

Address, City, State, Zip:

Home Phone: Office Phone:

E-mail: Birthday: